Lazy Traveller Blog

MICHAEL NOONAN

DEDICATION

I want to thank Cornelia for planning the Myanmar journey, for making so many good decisions and for being such a good companion.

Lazy Traveller Blog 1

I am on a flight from Bahrain to Bangkok. It is 2030 UK time. I woke up this morning at 0500 after a short night with no sleep. I have just finished a very good meal of sweet and sour humour, which is a local fish served with stir-fried Chinese noodles and mixed vegetables. The fish was delicious but the second glass of red wine was probably more than I needed. I am feeling merry and slightly stupid.

Ciara set a high standard for blogs on her round the world trip last year or the year before. I can't compete. I have never blogged before and I am not sure I have anything to say but it may be a good experiment to try to write a note each day during this trip to Asia and see what happens to the lazy traveller.

I was not sure I was going to get away from the UK at all today. I tried to check in online yesterday morning and found that Gulf Air did not allow online check ins at Heathrow. I had just an email note from Ebookers with a number. I had not registered with Gulf Air at all and I had not given my passport details to anyone. I was not sure that I was not going to get to the airport and be turned away. If I was travelling alone I don't think I would have minded. I could have crept back to London quietly and told very few that I had not managed after all to get away. I could have hidden away quietly for four weeks and pretended at the end that I had done this journey to Thailand, Burma and Cambodia and no one would have been any the wiser. I would have been a very lazy traveller. As it was, I had no problems and I am in the air. All worked out well despite my lack of planning and preparation. I got to Heathrow by 0700 and check in was easy and we left perhaps an hour late but by that time I was writing on my netbook and oblivious to what was happening around me.

The first leg of the journey went well. I had a change of plane in Bahrain and when I got on this flight I thought I should dip into the guidebook on Bangkok which Tim and Reid had lent to me. I was going to check some details about the location of the hotel, which has been arranged for me by Cornelia and get some hints about how to get from the airport to the hotel. When I looked into the guidebook that was when I realised I should be called the lazy traveller. This was a moment of revelation and terror. I have arranged a visa for my trips to Cambodia and Burma. Rachel directed me to get an online visa for Cambodia and it arrived by email on Monday evening, a few days after I finally completed the online application. Laziness is also about being late and deferring everything to the last moment. Reid advised me about the Burmese visa and I sorted that out a few weeks ago. It all went well.

But I realised however I had not bothered to think about Thailand and getting a visa to get into the country. I have visited a number of times before and I have no recall of arranging or applying for visas. I hope I don't need one in the morning when I get off the plane. We will see. I hope I don't need passport pics for a visa which the authorities may want at the border. I have none (although Cornelia advised that I should have a few ready just in case. Cornelia is a planner and she is not a lazy traveller). I am hoping, perhaps foolishly, that all will be well when I arrive tomorrow morning just as all was well when I checked in. This is foolishness and laziness in practice.

I am going along for the trip in blind ignorance and have not done much preparation and planning. Cornelia has planned every step of our Burmese adventures and I am sure all will go like clockwork and all the details will work out perfectly. She has even managed to arrange for travel insurance and has had the right jabs and is ready with malaria tablets and antibiotics. I have done none of this. I am a careless and lazy traveller waiting for my nemesis. I am barely packed and I travel very lightly.

I am a "Candide" character in this world of foreign adventure, still naively believing in the best of all possible worlds. And I continue to believe in this naive world view because nothing too bad has, as yet, happened. And I hope nothing will.

Tim's guidebook talks about the challenges of re-entry on a thirty-day tourist visa. I don't think I have encountered this problem before and I am not sure what the situation is. I will leave Thailand, assuming I am allowed in tomorrow morning, to go to Burma and then attempt to come back in, stay a few days before I leave for Cambodia. Then I do the same at the end of my visit there. That is the plan. But will it work? I am not sure now. If I manage to succeed in doing this I will have entered and left Thailand three times in 28 days. I wonder if the border officials will allow this. I think now I should have checked this before I left the UK. I did not. And now the position is more intriguing. I hope all will be well. I am not keen to discover the inside of a Thai jail or be sent back on a light back to the UK at my own expense. I live in naïve and foolish hope.

If I manage to get into Thailand today and if I manage to find my hotel I am hoping there will be a travel agent tomorrow who can advise me and let me know if I need to do anything to keep the border control authorities happy. I know that if I was a foreigner trying to do this in the UK I might have problems. Laziness is beginning to feel like a stupid option. I sense that I can solve this problem and this problem is all in my mind. There will be an easy solution.

I thought I would find my hotel in the guidebook and I would get a hint of how to get there because I forgot to get directions from the website last night. I was too busy sending out notes on projects to people I won't be able to contact for a while. Now it seems it would have been a good idea to check the location of the hotel and be a bit clearer on where it is. I have a booking form with an address. Cornelia booked it for me. It is a good hotel and I am quietly, but naively, confident that at the airport there will be an information desk which can give me some hints and tips about how to make my way from the airport to the hotel. Although I will be tired at that stage, assuming I have been allowed in to the country, it is early in the morning and I am in no great hurry. This is a big country and the hotel where I am staying is a big one. I think, perhaps foolishly, I will find my way and all will be well.

I remember how much preparation Ciara put into her round the world journey. I am awed by the care Cornelia has put into the Burmese part of the journey. I am only overwhelmed by the lack of planning I have done for this trip. I am not sure at this point that this is the right approach. A certain amount of careful planning would reduce the anxiety and ambiguity I am feeling at the moment.

But I am fairly confident in a naive and foolish way that I will get into the country, I will find my hotel without too much anguish, that the hotel will be fine, that Cornelia and I will connect as we should and we will have a splendid time. And that none of these concerns which seem so pressing at this point will turn into major issues. I have grown into a lazy traveller because things in the past have usually worked out well. I have ripened into a lazy traveller as a smelly cheese matures into well rounded ripeness. In the past, and perhaps when I first came to Thailand in 1989, I suspect I planned a lot more. It is a long time ago. Now I assume that all will probably be well, there will be people who are willing to help. If I ask the right question I will find an answer. I usually find what I need and practicalities will sort themselves out without much problem. The world is not a fearful or dangerous place most of the time. I hope this trip will prove me wrong.

No matter what happens, based on my understanding of these silly dilemmas, I resolve to be less lazy in the future in terms of checking out the visa situation, knowing how to make my way to my hotel and getting an up to date guidebook.

Meanwhile, alongside eating the pleasant fish and drinking too much wine, I have been reading act 1 of Richard III, an amazing history play with Shakespeare in top gear, so to speak. In this act we meet Richard, who is the Duke of Gloucester and the younger brother of the Yorkist king, Edward IV. He tells us that he intends to plot against both his brothers and arrange to murder the Duke of Clarence, his brother, the Queen's entire family and the issue of both their families (the princes in the tower), and since the king is sickly this will ensure he becomes king. He is a villainous, immoral figure of intrigue, vice and deceit. Margaret of Anjou, whom we have come to know from Henry VI parts 2 and 3 curses every member of the Yorkist dynasty and damns them to hell for murdering her husband, Henry VI and her son, Prince Edward. We see Richard send murderers to kill his brother, the Duke of Clarence, in the Tower. Clarence attempts to convince the murderers that it could not have been Gloucester who gave the order for his death but we and the murderers know that Richard is responsible. Heady stuff for a flight between Bahrain and Bangkok.

Time to sleep. Tomorrow I will tell the story of what happened at the airport and the next hesitant steps of the lazy traveller in Asia.

Just to keep you up to speed:
The visas are all ok
The hotel is fantastic
Everything is working out fine and all the issues have been solved.
Time for bed.

stop, that taste so good ... and the taste continues
...a few notes of the gamelan, a tapping, a strong
rhythm—you musicians, so warm and so contained in your skill
music the fruit you know

music the mango. who can forget it,
exuberant, how it pushes through
against and just before it falls into over ripening. you have seduced it

deliciously it has tamed you with its taste

music the mango. the tropical climate—
play it out of you, allow it to sweat
in the heat of its homeland. abounding in the physical of glory
peel away

layer of scent after scent and colour. create your own connection
with the luscious, gently reluctant peel
and sweet juice its vitality drips a joyful succulence

    (Bangkok, 2nd March 2012)
    Adapted from Rilke's poem on the orange

Lazy Traveller Blog 2

I have just eaten a plate of pad thai with prawns and I am now having a cup of tea looking out over the vibrant city around the hotel. All is going well.

My laziness all resolved itself well today. The anxieties of yesterday's flight from Bahrain were all solved neatly and effortlessly with the help of those around me.

At the airport this morning a lot of people were a bit confused about the visa situation for British passports. But a Spanish social worker from Valencia working in Hammersmith and Fulham and me talked to a young Thai woman who was on the information desk and she confirmed that we did not need a visa and we could reenter the country as many times as we wished. I could enter Thailand and then leave for Burma and Cambodia and still get back in. My anxieties on the flight about this were groundless. They had been increased however when landing cards were distributed and they included a section for visa number. I already saw myself locked in a room for hours waiting to be told at the end the flight that I was going fly back to the UK on and having to explain to Cornelia that I had not managed to get into the country after all. That problem was resolved.

I want to focus on a few things which surprised me today and proved to be delightful.

When I picked up my luggage and changed some dollars for baht at the airport I tried to find how to make my way into the city centre and the hotel. A man from the hotel was willing to arrange a luxurious taxi for me but it was going to cost around 2,000 baht. That did not seem the right thing to do. Instead I asked him for advice on how I could make my way to the hotel, which he knew, without use of the limousine. He not only told me the route using a new high speed link between the airport and the city centre (equivalent to the Heathrow Express) but he took me through the labyrinth of the airport, helped me purchase an express ticket and got me to the right platform. He was not going to make any commission for helping me but he was a kind and ministering angel. And by this time I was flagging.

The train was very smart and modern and left on time. It took seventeen minutes to get from the airport to the centre of the city and cost 90 baht or two pounds and was an interesting experience. Public transport feels appropriate for a lazy traveller. This connection was not here when I last visited Bangkok in 1993, on my way back from Japan. Yesterday on the train into the city I had the impression that the country had completed a lot of huge public transport projects. I remember bad traffic queues in Bangkok, roads permanently clogged, huge crossroads and a filthy smog hovering over the roads and sidewalks, partly caused by belching fumes from the tuk tuks and huge lorries rushing close by the open shops and stalls along the streets.

Sitting on the train, now wondering how I was going to make the connection from the airport fast speed link to the sky train, a man started to talk to me who wanted to practise his English and when I said where I was trying to get to, he said he would help me because he was heading for a station on the same line but much further out. The lazy traveller had met another angel. He talked about Thai politics and economics, strong government, problems in the city, the ASEAN countries and the advantages of Thailand. He told me about his eldest son who is a doing a degree course in international engineering and that his undergraduate degree will cost his father 1.5 million baht (£30k). This is the same story we are working out in the UK with university fees. Each evening over dinner with the family they have fifteen minutes of English to help one another. The father, another angel, had been in the Thai air force and was now something in security with the Bank of Thailand. He gave me his card and offered further help if I needed it before I left for Burma. He helped me off the fast speed train, showed me where the transit system commenced, helped me to get change and buy a ticket (now I know how to do this) and to make a transfer. The sky train dropped me a few minutes from my hotel. No doubt the limousine would have been easier but I would have missed out on the ministering angels and getting to talk with ordinary Thai people. I enjoyed my journey into town and can do it next time on my own.

These ministering angels were a wonderful surprise and I enjoyed their support. I wonder if visitors to the UK are greeted by people as willing to help them.

The hotel was a different sort of surprise. I had forgotten how lavish Asian hotels can be, how huge the rooms can be, how beautiful the bathrooms, how many beautiful lamps and fittings. The lobby is an amazing space filled with flowers and fine art. My room is on the seventh floor and looks down onto an internal terrace with a Thai courtyard garden on the ground floor and a fish pool full of carp. I was a bit overwhelmed by the luxuriousness of the room and the hotel and I felt initially as a crumpled and now shaven traveller a bit out of place. Asia and Thailand have immense wealth. Some of the hotel's wealth is geared at international business but most people in the huge atrium are Thai and Asian people who are clearly very wealthy. The lobby is full of beautiful flowers and traditionally inspired works of art. This is a beautiful space to sit and people watch. The lazy traveller will find it very easy to be lazy over tea while watching people in this space.

This sort of wealth and lavish luxury is slightly uncomfortable however. It is pleasant but I don't have a sense that I am in the right place. There have always been wonderful and wealthy hotels in Bangkok but this was not my richest or most abiding impression of the city in the past.

I slept for a few hours and then headed out when the city had cooled off slightly around 1430. As part of my laziness I do not try to get to know a city with a map nor with a list of things I want to do. I enjoy just wandering aimlessly for a day at least, not entirely clear where I am heading to, if indeed, I am heading anywhere. The goal is to wander, to see, to be surprised and to gain a solid but grounded impression of what is going on, how life is led. Wandering is a great way of being surprised. This sort of aimless wandering in a new city, or even in a city one used to know but which has changed is a great pleasure.

The hotel is on a big highway opposite the sky train and the areas is full of new shopping centres and more beautiful hotels. These building, with the amazing tall office blocks and multiple layered highways are the new face of a very confident Thailand which sees itself as a centre for the ASEAN countries and a conduit for trade between China and the ASEAN countries. And this city wants to be cosmopolitan, open, diverse, tolerant, welcoming, functional, efficient while still charming and interesting. I don't know if the plan will work but I am amazed by the changes I can see in Thailand; the city is vibrant, rich and cosmopolitan in a way unlike any city in UK. This new Bangkok is a confident, outward looking business-focused regional trading centre. And it is founded on enterprise, business, marketing, consumption, trade and goods. Asia still feels glittering and bounteous in terms of its wealth of goods and things. I was being asked about the problems in Greece and how these problems were likely to impact the UK. The implication was that these problems with an environment of cuts are not what is happening in Asia at the moment.

One image of the Buddha is of a fat, wealthy older man laughing, revelling in long life, happiness and contentment. He glories in the abundance of wealth, good food, a large family and the good things of the world. He leads a good life and is almost a contemporary business leader and happy grandfather who has neglected any visits to the gym. This is the Buddha of wealth, happiness and contentment which presides over contemporary glitzy Bangkok. This wealthy city is admirable and very attractive but it is also intimidating. You have to be in the right circles of power and wealth to enter this realm and to play a role. The big international dazzling hotels in Thailand, and elsewhere in Asia, are places where the people who have this wealth come to circulate, display themselves and make connections. As a visitor I can hover on the edge of this world, be amazed and wonder at it, see its intimidating dazzle but I realise I am not part of this world.

It is a shock to be translated from my life in London, working now in the cultural and not for profit sector, and land in this new Thai Dallas. It is disconcerting but very enjoyable. I am on vacation and have ended up in Paradise.

This paradise hotel will be the base I come back to after my trips to Burma and Cambodia. I am going to get to know it better.

Another one of the many surprises today was to walk along the streets outside the hotel and move just a few blocks away from the new five-star hotels and find close by the old Bangkok that I remember from earlier trips. It still exists after all and has not been lost. I had forgotten this dirty and noisy city but suddenly I stumbled across it by accident. Old shops, quite small and each owned and run by a family opening directly onto the streets are still there. The sidewalks are noisy, filthy, uneven and very crowded. There are sidewalk stalls with wonderful displays of goods selling everything and anything. There are road side eating places which fill the streets with delicious smells. These pleasant and exotic smells are immediately redolent of the Bangkok I knew from the past. It was a very pleasant surprise to find that this dirty, less glitzy, noisy and exuberant city is still here. The powerful and inviting smells are still here, the local shrines are still here, the food stalls are still here, the tuk tuk drivers are still here. This old shabby but welcoming and slightly seedy city has continued while the new more glitzy city has appeared alongside it. These cities feel like very different worlds and foreign tourists move between them. It is very enjoyable to wander along these streets and just take them in. This is a city of knock off bargains and cheap imitations, avid bartering, small family firms, strange translations and delicious local food. This is the Bangkok I remember from my earlier trips.

An old lady with a straw hat and a very large welcoming smile was selling delicious warm soft bread sandwiches filled with delicious bright green bean paste. High school students just let out of school were buying them from her for ten baht. She was an old lady and this was her pitch at the side of the road, a small cart served as a steam oven or heater. She had no English but it was a pleasure to taste what she was selling.

As if spanning these two different worlds there is a local shrine, not even a temple, next to the Erawan hotel at a huge intersection. It was filled with people of all ages, and many young people including many men, offering sweet smelling flower garlands of jasmine flowers and burning incense sticks to the gold image which was laden with gifts, thousands of yellow sweet smelling flower blossoms and offerings. This four-faced figure with eight arms in a mirrored niche enjoys receiving nice things from worshippers, enjoys sweet smells, brilliant flower heads, figures of elephants, the smell of incense and being asked for help. Under a canopy protected from the sun a three-person Thai band with wooden gamelans and a drum was playing music while a group of eight female dancers in traditional Thai costume, with large headdresses and complex dresses, danced when the worshippers had made the right contributions. The worshippers knelt on cushions in front of the musicians and dancers offering worship to the image while the dancers and musicians entertained the god. This was like crowd sourcing for worship and religious ritual. These gods know how to live well. It was good to stand back and record a minute or two of this wonderful music and the delicate movements.

A traditional Thai way of life has retained some small peripheral role despite the rapid westernisation. It seems just sidelined and minuscule but it was interesting to watch the sheer number of people making offerings and see the reverence with which they perform the rituals, holding up incense and bowing before the image.

Outside the shrine in front of a big department store, another group of contemporary musicians using some traditional instruments had adapted traditional music and were giving it a modern twist. I recorded a short extract of them playing.

I remember first coming to Thailand in the late 80s and relishing the cheap shopping. It represented abundance. The side streets away from the big malls full of branded goods are still full of such shops and huge messy shopping complexes piled high with cheap goods and abundance. Yesterday these places were full of local people and few foreigners. The country then was welcoming, open and easy to live in. There was no harassment on the streets and there was a busy spirit of tolerance and acceptance. This Bangkok is still here and it is a spirit which you don't find all over Asia. It is good to find it again. It is so different from anything we have in Europe and remains alluring, exotic and foreign.

This is a country with many layers and it is rich, very alluring and full of surprises.

And the pad thai was good.

Lazy Traveller Blog 3

I started the day with congee (rice porridge) and chicken, finished off with some green leaves and soy sauce. Delicious, especially when combined with coffee and an English muffin.

I was not sure what to do initially. I wanted to wander over to see a temple and perhaps visit the National Museum, because I don't think I ever visited this place in the past. Carol Graham has written a new book for American students about to go abroad for a year or two to study. Her advice is not to do "cultural" stuff but to get into a circle of people who share passions and interests of your own. When I heard her advice I realised I have been travelling in the wrong way for years. No matter.

I am fascinated to see how many people have iPads in Thailand and to see how they are using them. They have become a life accessory. I saw a man having breakfast across from me working away on his emails and reading newspapers on his iPad while waiting for his wife and daughter to appear. I thought I would ask his advice on how to get from where I was near the hotel to somewhere near the National Museum. A man with an iPad has the world of knowledge at his fingertips.

He did not have a clue and had no idea where the place was, even when I pulled out a high-level map and showed it to him. I was probably like a Japanese tourist in London stopping someone on the street and showing them a map in Japanese and asking directions. He was as clueless as we are. Perhaps it is not called the National Museum in Thai. When I got there later I realised it was full of Thai schoolchildren and a few stray foreign tourists. The man in the coffee shop did not have a clue but at that point his wife came to the rescue and she came up with a great plan. I should take the sky train from Siam to Taksim and catch a boat along the Chao Phraya river to the stop for the National Museum. Wow! That was a killer of a plan, almost made for me and she knew it worked.

I set off fired up with enthusiasm. There are now high level pedestrian walkways running over the big roads in downtown Bangkok, on the model of those previously in Hong Kong and Singapore, perfect for keeping dry during heavy tropical storms and out of the sun during the heat of the day. I don't remember them in Bangkok in the past. One of these walkways was outside where I was having breakfast and I walked to the Siam station, fascinated at all I could see from the walkway and people heading off to business. I caught the sky train to Taksim, the station on the riverside.

The river service was all new to me. There was an amazing array of tickets to bamboozle a lazy tourist but I found one for thirty bahts which would take me along the river on an express boat. This was an amazing trip and my first delight of the day. It was a lovely morning. The river at the moment is very high; it is wide as it snakes gloriously through the city.

From the boat I could see various palaces, temples, hotels and amazing new luxury apartment buildings on the riverside.

First stop was the Oriental Hotel, where Alain has recommended we go for dinner or tea. I will suggest that to Cornelia when she arrives tomorrow evening. This river trip was a great way to start the day and to recover a sense of the city. Although I must have crossed the river when I was here in the past to go to Wat Arun, I don't remember going on one of these trips down the Chao Phraya. One time I was here there was a Buddhist celebration of the dead, which involved sailing at night small paper lotus blossoms, with a tea light inside, down the Chao Phraya. These boats commemorated the dead and consigned their souls to the river. I got on a small narrow boat to see from the river the fireworks which were part of the same celebration. I remember then how fragile these little boats are and how immense and powerful the river seems when you are in a small boat.

The river boat this morning called in at six stops or so on the river. A largish, very red older western man got on at the same stop and I started to talk to him. His name was John Henshall and he came from Vancouver in Canada. He has been travelling around the world since November and he said he celebrated his 66th birthday a few weeks ago in Australia. He left Vancouver in November and had visited Beijing, Kuala Lumpur, Singapore before a long spell in Australia, visiting Adelaide and Sydney and now was heading back to Canada via Asia. Bangkok had overwhelmed him. He is due back in Vancouver next week. This was the last stage of his trip and he was staying at an International Hostel in the centre of Bangkok. I liked his freedom to travel and the pleasure he had found in each of the countries he had visited. He was relishing his journey and had an appetite for more. He was a man with an iPad and said he had already taken eight hundred or so photos from his trip. He looked very red and not very well so I did not like to ask why he was making this trip at this time and what was his sense of urgency. I said almost jokingly that when he got back to Vancouver he could start to plan his next trip. But it was not a joke. He had started to plan it already and he will be in New Zealand next Christmas. He has caught the travelling bug and he is now a modern pilgrim and a silver wayfarer. He had a DK guidebook and told me what he had seen and what he intended to see. He had a plan to visit the weekend markets tomorrow and was enjoying the city a lot. The evening before he had enjoyed a Thai meal and he said he was on a mission now to find the same sort of Thai cuisine back in Vancouver. The trip was clearly transformative in many ways for him.

We chatted and I helped him on his way when we got off the boat at a stop called Phra Athit pier next to the modern bridge which spans the river. He was ready to sit down, have a drink and make some notes. I was ready to wander.

The river was so attractive and an unexpected delight. It looked amazing at this early time of the morning before the sun became very strong and while there was only a small number of passengers. This boat was an express ferry and was clearly only used by foreigners. The local people had other solutions to get up and down the river. The Buddhist Thai temples face onto the river. Either they are constructed as a huge tall pointed stupa shape with multiple layers or they are built in the shape of a house with amazing gold edged eaves. The roofs sparkle in the sunshine and the gold on the temples dazzle as gold is intended to do. They attract pilgrims and visitors with their shapes and allure. Wat Arun is the Temple of the Dawn and faces across to the Royal Palace and the main Temple complex. There is a lot to see and enjoy.

I was vaguely heading for the National Museum and walked in that direction back towards the centre of the city when I got off the boat but after a while and a few fascinating detours I needed to ask for a direction and I was sent back the way I came. I had followed a path along the riverside because it looked so tantalising and so it proved. The path went through a huge university campus fronting onto the river and led eventually into an old market selling vast amounts of Buddhist religious statues and paraphernalia. I am not sure of the various streams of Buddhism. These artefacts were not images of the Buddha but images of wise old men who were saints and teachers, I think. These were gnarled figures of old wizened scholars who had managed to transform the pollen of their time into something like honey or amber in terms of their life and teaching. I was intrigued. These are wise old men and most of them have a sweet smile of contentment and celebration as if they found the secret of how to live. They hold out a promise of a wise content old age if you follow the path to truth. They did not have the belly laugh of the laughing Buddha but still they had found a secret. These are not figures we celebrate in the Western tradition and I took pictures of a few of these figures.

Another wrong turn led me to wander into a meditation centre which I thought might be the National Museum. I was intrigued and curious. The trees around the meditation halls contained a bird with an amazing call. I tried to catch it with my video camera but by the time I switched the camera on, the bird had finished its song. The main meditation hall, was full of people either sitting silently in meditation or walking around a small space very, very slowly and attentively in a form of walking meditation. Fascinating stuff, with plenty of people and activity quite unlike the temple in the afternoon.

I found the National Museum and wandered past a lot of displays telling me the story of Thailand. They did not quite do it for me. This Museum used to be the Front Palace, occupied by a member of the Royal Family. It was full of children who were on school trips and wanted to talk to me and made a good attempt but then ran away in trepidation when I replied to them. They were great fun. The museum had a number of high points. The internal courtyard gardens of the palace with inner pools and fish were a delight. These were lovely courtly spaces but apart from these courtyards the palace did not have gardens.

There was a huge audience chamber which had become a temple or perhaps it was always a temple, called the Buddhaisawan Chapel. On the lower levels the walls were covered with murals telling stories of the gods, full of narrative details, of exquisite quality and coming from a school of Thai painting which the Four Seasons has taken as a device for decorating the hotel. However, this chapel contained the real thing. It is a style quite different from Indian miniature painting and very different from Chinese and Japanese forms of painting. The characters are realistic and delightful and the settings are rich and lively. I have taken some pictures. The decoration of the whole chapel was on five levels, the upper four levels above the scenes contain layered series of wise figures, gods and angels lining up in the direction of the end of the chapel to watch and adore. It was wonderful. The walls of the temple on multiple layers are like the contemporary highways across the city having pedestrian walk ways, sky trains and roads.

The central halls of the museum were filled with royal and religious paraphernalia and there was a room of Thai and Asian musical instruments but these objects although fascinating were now lifeless. These were props and the props were lifeless when separated from the ritual and life they were designed to enhance and accompany. There was a room of delightful puppets and shadow puppets but no puppet show. I was left wanting more. One room was packed full of musical instruments but it was silent. I wanted to hear the instruments come alive and hear the sounds of this amazing court orchestra. There were rooms of palanquins and funerary chariots to carry the live and dead royal bodies from the palace around the city and eventually to the location of cremation. The funerary chariots contained the body in a life sized funeral urn or jar. But these objects only come to life as part of an amazing ritual. The museum contained some grainy photographs but no video footage. This part of the museum contained just shadows of life and the peripherals of culture in Thailand but the life of the city and country was not present in the objects.

On the other hand, there was a lot of Buddhist and religious statuary of amazing quality and this was a different sort of experience. These are mainly human figures, usually alone, in a heightened state of contemplation, peace or wisdom. They are from various times, in various different styles and all of a very high quality. It is interesting to look at so many; I was impressed by the vast array and its diversity. They all told of human vitality. It is if these are exercises in positive and healthy narcissism. The artists look into the looking glass of perfection and they see themselves, a human form translated into the ideal. Art and religion reflect the best of humanity, or reflect here the sweet and rich taste of consciousness. The sculptors project into stone and wood the best and wildest aspects of their own humanity; viewing them was a rich and life affirming experience. These figures are not tortured and they do not suffer need even when they are old. They are figured in which the civil war of need and anxiety has come to an end or a permanent truce. They have broken through the narrowing confines of the personal and limited consciousness and the will. They have tasted their own consciousness and it is sweet and good. They are enlightened. This is what it looks like for a person to become the Buddha. They had burnt off the fumes of desire and the will to power and they are left with an enlightenment of receptivity and grace. This is an art of human celebration. It is not unworldly and does not despise the world or the body. It celebrates the human in its most contemplative and radiant aspects. But if these are images of realised consciousness, beyond desire and anxiety, they are solely states of consciousness, moments of being. It is hard to believe that these figures could enter into the drama of everyday life or the plays of Shakespeare. These works of art and religion are works of a contemplative art realised in stone and wood.

The images are displayed in a museum but this is religious art aiming at some specific transformation and having a specific purpose. Such art is designed to touch, to appeal, to evoke and to draw a response. It is designed for worshippers and designed to stimulate and inspire devotees. I was touched and enjoyed the experience a lot. I don't know how I might have responded if I had seen these statues in the British Museum. This was a good place to see them come to life and feel their power. This was an old-style museum and these objects, if not neglected, seemed to be forgotten treasures, left to their own devices and hidden away as great treasures because they were such high quality. But they are quite distinct from the faces I see on the street, especially the faces hunting for bargains and making deals in the night markets around the city.

There was only one figure of a boddhisattva. The rest of the figures were monks and images of the Buddha.

The last pleasure of the day was a noisy temple on the far bank of the Chao Phraya. I had not intended to visit it but the boat docked nearby and I saw on the landing stage people sitting down with drinks. I was thirsty and decided to jump off and see what might be able to drink close by. But the coffee shops were not so attractive when I walked around them. The landing stage was filled with market stall selling clothes. But I was hot and not in the mood for shopping. I wandered off to the temple which I had seen from the river. On the way I spotted a middle-aged man playing an instrument plaintively with a small cup in front of him for offerings. The sound was harsh and rough but it was still very beautiful, although tuneless. It was a good moment and I recorded a quick snatch of his music on my camera. Near the landing stage there was a young woman playing a stringed instrument like a cimbalom with a little hammer. She played very beautifully.

The temple had its own landing stage from the river with steps leading up from the river, perhaps used to deposit dead bodies into the river at some stage. The area was filled with people throwing soft brown bread rolls to the pigeons. Or I thought they were feeding the pigeons but when I looked down they were feeding a vast shoal of gigantic fish which were all eager for the scraps of bread rolls. Around the people throwing bread was a seething mass of dark grey pigeons and below a dense shoal of huge fish with mouths open leaping out to grab the pieces of bread. This must be deeply symbolic in some way but it was all rather curious and full of life. The river must be clean enough for these fish to survive and thrive.

The route between the river and the temple was lined with disabled and very old people selling lottery tickets and temple garlands made of jasmine and yellow flower heads. Inside the temple compound there was enormous activity everywhere. This was a temple like a Disney park full of ways for people to participate in various ritual activity.

Monks lined up on plastic chairs inside the temple gate were using microphones for some reason, perhaps saying prayers over the saffron robes people were offering to them. The worshippers made the monks an offering of these saffron robes wrapped up in plastic bags; the monks then seemed to give back the robes with a note which had been written by a man behind the scenes in a form of calligraphy. I did not understand what was happening but I was fascinated. In other chapels on either side of the gate there was more activity while outside people were lighting incense sticks wrapped in flower garlands and then offering these incense smells to the images while touching their foreheads with the smoking incense. In an area away from the main temples worshippers could pay to sound a series of bells, which had been hung around a stall. This was fascinating and the sounds all these bells sounded as multiple worshippers went on their way striking the bells was wonderful. tried to catch the sound on film but I am not sure it will come out. Behind this area a monk was reciting sutras while he held in front of his face a large leaf with a photograph of someone. On the table next to this monk reciting sutras a large overweight monk in his robes was watching boxing on a large flat TV screen with two other guys.

In another area there were floating votive lamps. People were provided with ladles and they scooped the oil from around the floating lamp or wick and further fuelled the flame in clockwise circles. It all seemed very mysterious and fascinating. I was taken by all of this activity. Down a small alley there was a man who was standing as if he was in a coma, completely rigid and staring wildly in front of him. No one approached him and he seemed as much at one with the place as the man in black hosing down the pavement at the back either at work or atoning for some error in this or another life.

In the main temple hall people came in, knelt down and saluted the image by prostrating themselves three times bringing their hands together in a Namaste gesture, kissing them and then laying their hands down on the floor and then placing their foreheads on their outstretched hands. This was a very different gesture from the one made with incense offerings at the shrine near my hotel. Everyone seemed to do it in the same way and in many ways it is very like the Islam form of prayer in a mosque (but without the hand movement behind the ears). The prostration is a very physical act of worship. The women did it with great gravity. The men did it hurriedly and cursorily. The hall was full of couples and young families coming with their children. They stayed a few minutes to salute the Buddha, as a great ancestor one visits from time to time and who lives in a grand but darkened room set apart from the main activity of the house and then they left with their duties all done. It seemed a genial form of visit. But there were also people who having worshipped were then chatting to friends on their mobiles, or they took pictures of one another, posing in front of granddad Buddha, or others were using their iPads to take photographs for the folks back in the office. This local temple was full of activity and lots of participation.

And the temple itself joined in, singing sweetly. From the eaves of the temple roof bells and chimes were hanging which were blown by and sounded in the wind. It was an enchanting experience to walk around the temple filled with this gentle music, a music of the wind, like the music which enchants Caliban on his island in the Tempest. None of the images at this temple were particularly good or moving and the buildings themselves were not of a high quality but the local community of worshippers filled this place with amazing and rich forms of activity. It was a real delight to watch and to enjoy all that was going on and to see one form of the culture brought to life in this place. It was fascinating.

Lazy Traveller Blog 4

All is going well. It is now Sunday evening. Cornelia is flying in within the next 1.5 hours and the next stage of our journey will start in the morning when we fly from Bangkok to Rangoon/Yangon. The next stage will be quite different from these few days in Bangkok which have been very enjoyable.

Last night, after visiting the royal collection Buddhas, I was visited by jet lag demons in the middle of the night. I had to get up and write for an hour or so and then fall asleep. A knock at the door in the morning from housekeeping woke me and they asked if they could make up my room. It was around 1200. I had slept through the morning. Drats! I wanted to do so much today. But despite the demons and a late start, I managed to do at least three wonderful things. They are very touristy but still very enjoyable.

I wanted to visit the Royal Palace and see the Emerald Buddha, visit the huge monastery next to the Royal Palace (also called Wat Phra Kaew and Grand Palace), Wat Pho, catch up with the giant reclining Buddha and possibly cross the Chao Phrao to visit Wat Arun the temple of the Dawn, somewhat ironically around sunset. I managed to do all this but I am now running out of time to write before Cornelia arrives.

Wat Pho is a huge temple complex next to the Royal Palace. It has been a centre of learning and education for a long time. You can do courses in Thai massage and Thai medicine there and the students are looking for tourists to try their skills on. The monastery seems to divide into two spaces. One space immediately inside the front gate is dedicated to the giant reclining Buddha and the other space is the rest of the monastery and quite distinct. I visited them in reverse order.

As I started to walk around this monastery complex I remembered I had visited here before on my first visit to Thailand in 1989 but at that stage this complex had not been refurbished and the courtyards featuring multiple images of the Buddha praying were dark and overcast, dark and perhaps neglected with the grime of centuries. That has all changed. Now the walls are white, the statues are golden and everything is sparklingly clean and stunning. It is a strange combination of unusual structures and shapes and multiple versions of the Buddha. It is a bit confusing have a figure replicated perhaps hundred times. This is a different aesthetic from the one in the west focused on individuality and uniqueness. Each of these praying Buddhas was an individual work. This was not a project like the Xian warriors with manufactured bodies with stick-on individualised heads. Each was special and yet there was no striving for personality. Personality and the individual had been taken out of the equation. And when this goes it is hard to understand why there are so many of the same thing, as if multiplicity changes the value of something. If there is one or perhaps a few we have enough attention to give to the individual objects and we can value them with our time. When there are so many and the distinctions from one to the others are so slight, it is hard to concentrate on any individual thing. Instead we step back and notice an overall impression. In some way we are fazed and dazzled by the sheer number of these things. They are meant to impress perhaps in terms of their number and then impress individually in terms of their quality I was reminded of Circe who translates her lovers into stone. It was as if all these Buddhas had once existed and had been monks in this place. They had been transformed into everlasting adoring disciples in this place. Christianity has the concept of a heaven in which the saints praise and adore God. This is a Buddhist vision of something similar, perhaps. These statues are frozen courtiers at the court of a high sovereign. Impact and drama were created by the sheer number of the objects, the setting and their golden skin. In other places this amount of replication might be seen as a response to doubt but that did not seem an issue here. Instead it was as if this was an attempt to replicate on earth and in Bangkok some concept of a heaven or a royal and religious court to prove that heaven was indeed here in this city at the time when this was all created and then forever more. For such a religious outlook it was strange to see that numbers were so important and that there was such discipline and exactitude. Individuality and personality had been taken out of the system.

Of course in a pre-industrial environment reproduction and sameness are miracles, dazzling to see that one thing can be replicated again and again and each looks like the rest. It is a miracle of a sort we lost with industrial processes of production where uniformity became the norm. And with that we changed our values. We are no longer surprised and amazed by multiplicity. We expect sameness with ordinary things and uniqueness in special areas such as art or religion. This temple disturbs these expectations and leaves us slightly confused.

It was also clear that the model for much of the iconography was mainly Indian although there were also figures from China, such as the Confucian scholars and the twelve animals you find represented on royal avenues in China. Or perhaps all these ideas originate in India.

The fingers and hand gestures of the Buddha were the only means to indicate shades of meaning. And this translates from Buddhist sculpture to dance and ritual, in which the hands are used in a very stylised manner whereas the face is often covered in a mask or painted. In another location there was a series of pictures showing the Buddha on different days of the week, governed by different planets in different poses, wearing different colours and displaying various hand gestures associated with each day. This was the first time I had seen this explicated but I could not photograph it.

It was also interesting that in these monastic places the only dramatic figures are the watchmen and guardians, who are stern figures standing at the threshold keeping evil forces outside the sacred spaces. In Japan these are the figures of wind and storm, earthquake and fire. Here they are huge ugly contorted guardians, almost demons. These figures stand guard but are not allowed into the sacred space. In Beijing there are certain Tibetan temples where such dark forces are given more space to be depicted—they are fascinating. Here these darker and more forceful energies are not allowed beyond the threshold with one exception, I think.

The monastery grounds were filled with courtyards of Buddhas, viewing halls and various stupas or prangs. Thai architecture does not develop the arch and does not seem to have the large viewing halls spanning nine spans which we find in China. These are dense spaces which grow upwards on straight columns and support hip roofed roves. I wished I had an architectural guide to explain what was occurring. The stupa shapes grow from a solid dense base and then each layer is less and less. The height is therefore governed by the mass at the base. Within this simple technology there is a huge project for grace and variation of decoration and attempts to lighten what is essential a solid and dull structure. Within the monastery the decoration is based on flat porcelain mosaics, representing flowers and vegetation.

The main object in this monastery is the Giant Reclining Buddha. The gigantic is another pre-industrial concept of power and mystery. This is a very large Buddha and I suppose it is reclining because it was easier to make a long, elongated structure in brick rather than a very high structure. This is a gigantic Buddha—perhaps ten times life size, beautifully proportioned and covered in gold leaf. It is a dazzling spectacle although since it is enclosed in a hall it is hard to see in its totality. We gasp at the stylised feet and toes on which various sutras have been written. But the gigantic has lost its power to give us an experience of awe and mystery, as it did in previous times. The gigantic of this sort is no longer imbued with fascination and mystery. It is interesting and it is a spectacle but I am not moved particularly because it is very large.

However, what seemed more interesting was that along the far side of the Buddha, the one with his back, there were multiple bronze bowls and a ritual has developed of dropping metal coins into this series of bowls. The hall is filled with the delicate and beautiful sound of these coins dropping into the bowls. It is not until you get to the far end of the hall that a visitor realises this is the source of the musical sound. Gift giving and alms produce their own sound, the sound of offerings to the Buddha. There is clearly a strong correlation between money and worship. This is very strong in China and it is strong here. The god likes lots of money, likes receiving lots of money and worshippers like showing their worship by giving notes and coins. In the West we are now suspicious of the corruption of the church and the institution that we can no longer link the experience of money and the experience of the spiritual except for money to take away the mystique of the sacred. Money and capital are vital but they contaminate and detract from the religious. In this form of popular religion that fall of money from grace has not occurred. These gods like money and the monasteries collect money as they collect spiritual power—perhaps the two things are naively identified. Gods are powerful, just as people are powerful, because they are wealthy, they are blessed with bounty and beneficence. This ineffable and invisible power is evidenced and symbolised in money and most particularly in gold and things which contain light, things which glisten and delight the eye and the heart.

And so the giant reclining Buddha is covered in dazzling gold and the royal prangs in the Palace are covered in gold and the temples are covered in as much gold as possible. Gold indicates spiritual power. It would be nice if this was still the case but these tokens of power no longer directly affect us in the same power. The size of the Buddha and his gold covering did not dazzle me unduly but the sound of the coins rattling in the bronze bowls delighted, surprised and amazed me.

The Royal Palace was across the way from Wat Phrao. I had been told by someone who had stopped me on the street that the Royal Palace was closed until 1530 whereas it closed for entry at 1530. Although this is called a palace, the palace buildings are from 17th century and were not open to the public. The interest in this place is the religious buildings and relics which are attached to the palace. So why is this not a temple, although the buildings are religious and did not seem to have a courtly function (unlike say the Forbidden City with its various halls for imperial rituals)? The answer apparently is that a temple has monks attached to it. The monastery is a house for monks and their rituals determine the use of the fabric. There are no monks attached to these buildings and they are therefore just adjuncts to the Palace.

These are splendid and dazzling constructs full of dazzle, splendid decoration and gold aplenty. The shapes and constructions are the same as elsewhere so royal splendour and glory can only be indicated by glorious decoration and more lavish wealth. Royalty has to compete with religious power for dazzle and splendour. And it succeeds. In comparison with the wonderful decoration of these monuments the monastery next door looks subdued and severe in its monastic restraint. While the buildings and spaces seem the same there are new guardian figures here which are light airy constructs half male and half animal, half female and half bird. These are delightful surreal artefacts wonderfully realised, as light as airy and betokening a strange unearthly realm of legend.

Within the covered cloisters around this temple complex are depicted scenes from the Ramayana. This epic may also be used in the monasteries viewing halls but here the drama takes on a national and epic force. Within Buddhism the battle over the will and the appetites is internal. I am not sure that Buddha has advice for the wise ruler and king. The Ramayana, a Hindu epic, by contrast is a world governed by drama, battles, heroes, warriors and tests of courage. This is a mundane realm which can be used to depict and reflect national travails, conquest, suppression of foreign devils, usurpers, mythological battles of good and evil. We walk very close to these fascinating murals and they are as full of life and drama as the Buddhas in the monastery have been emptied of drama and tension. They must have been restored recently and they are in great condition. They are full of life, romances depicting battles with monkeys, elephants, monsters. I walked around the murals and enjoyed some of the details. I did not know the details of the story but it was easy to enjoy these pieces as a great work of art, depicting human triumphs and losses on a national and cosmic scale.

The centre piece of the Palace Complex is the emerald Buddha which is a small statue so small it is almost invisible. This statue is as fascinating as the Giant Buddha. The monks went for gigantism. The palace went for smallness and intensity. The Buddha does not seem emerald but this does not matter. It is an object which seems to symbolise the continuum of the state and religion, a link between Thailand and its religious heritage in India. It feels as if it holds the same status for Bangkok as the body of St Mark for Venice, or the body of Peter for Catholic Rome or perhaps the ravens and the tower of London. It is mystical symbol for the body of the state itself. It may be religious but it seems very magical (just as the Giant Buddha is magical and the hundreds of Buddhas remaining in eternal adoration are quite magical and elements of a pre-rational, pre-modern world. The statue of the Buddha sanctifies and justifies the country and the country gains its credibility and rationale from its protection of this relic. The symbol carries the weight of and signifies the lively and mythological reality the state.

It did not do anything for me but that was ok. I was already dazzled by all the buildings, the stupas, the demon and monkey guardians, the gold and floral decorations, the steps, the murals, the black bronze elephants and the model of Ankgor Wat. It was a wonderful experience.

On the marble floor outside the temple of the Emerald Buddha I met Maria from Valencia. What an amazing coincidence. We had sorted out the visa situation together when we arrived and then separated. We recognised one another suddenly and then spent some time catching up with what we had learnt about the city. She had done a lot more than I had. I realise I have slowed down in my sightseeing over the years. I am less hungry than I used to be. She leaves by train for a beach resort tonight. She was well and we took some photos. It was a lovely surprise.

I headed off to look at the rest of the palace and then headed across the river to visit Wat Arun. A small ferry took people from one side of the river to another. It was wonderful. Young boys were jumping of the ferry into the water and swimming around it. monks were going back to the monastery after a day on the other side of the river. There were local people and many tourists keen to visit Wat Arun before nightfall.

Wat Arun is a large prang on the far side of the Chao Phraya and was my last delight of the day. The Emerald Buddha used to be housed in a viewing hall within this complex until he was moved across to the Royal Palace.

The interest of Wat Arun for me, dedicated to the Hindu goddess of Dawn, is the decoration on the outside. There is no inside to this monument. It is a shape and an object in the landscape situated on the banks of the river. As with all these monuments they are just phallic shapes, symbols of generativity and miracles of pre-industrial engineering (although nowhere near as complex as a Gothic cathedral in terms of its engineering and devices). Visitors can climb up the steep stairs on the outside and reach various terraces. These towers are objects which enshrine the concept of mystical ascension and personal illumination, symbolising the step by step the soul needs to go through. The architectural elements are based on a mystical form of geometry with the number of terraces and steps between terraces representing different inner realties and planes.

In this case the external surfaces are encrusted with china plates and components which had been used as ballast on the boats coming into Thailand. It is an amazing surface, far more surreal than Gaudi's mosaic surfaces, in many ways. The plates and flowers made from plates dazzle on the surface. This is extravagant and beautiful nonsense and so a complete delight, pointless and joyous. Once I climbed up to third or fourth terrace. Today I climbed the first one and then decided I did not need to climb further. I was ready to climb down and get the ferry back to the hotel and get ready for Cornelia's arrival and our departure tomorrow for Burma.

I am not sure I will have email access in Burma. The lazy traveller may not be able to communicate for a while until he returns to Thailand.

Lazy Traveller Blog 5

Yangon, Myanmar, staying at Strand Hotel

Our first day in Myanmar but jet lag has caught up with me and I can hardly open my eyes.

We have arrived in Yangon, the old Rangoon. We went out for a walk around 1430 when the sun was not so intense. We spent a few hours walking around the city and making contact with people, being surprised by what we found.

What surprised us: The centre of the city was laid on a grid system by the British colonial power and the grid system is still in place.

The city is much poorer than Bangkok. There is amazing drive and resourcefulness and the people seem to be racially diverse with far more Indian people than I expected. The city feels as if it is thirty or forty years behind the times, at least. It is like stepping back in time but this does not feel like a good form of time travel. The people are poor, have very few

38

amenities and life is hard. This is like Brigadoon. If the main city is like this what must it be like in the country and in villages.

There is a thirty-minute time difference between Myanmar and Thailand. The flight took about ninety minutes and we flew with Bangkok Air. The immigration officer was fine and we had no problems with our visas at all.

Our hotel is on Strand Street and we are next to the British Embassy, on a main road. Across from us there is a street market with lots of produce and beyond that many large dockside warehouses and the river. We can't see the river and we have no sense that the city is built on the river.

There is a large Indian community here as well as the Burmese community and another Chinese community. These communities have separate areas within the city.

The centre of the city has remains of many old buildings, including buildings in mock Gothic, many art deco style buildings as well as classical, French and Anglo-Indian styles. I wonder how the buildings were selected. It is as if the designs came from a series of pattern books. The buildings look old and decrepit for the most part but still retain interesting shapes and will look very good some time in the future when the city receives a lot of money (from somewhere) to be regenerated.

The Strand Hotel where we are staying was built by the Raffles group in the 20s. It has had lots of famous visitors. It has huge public areas and large rooms with huge old fashioned bathrooms. The hotel looks out onto the British embassy. Our room and bathroom are vast and rather quaint in an old-fashioned way. Just like old Soviet hotels there are attentive butlers on each floor in national costume who look after us and appear when we arrive and leave. There are two dining rooms and the "fine" dining room is a splendid old fashioned room with silk lined chairs and a beautiful marble floor. When we walked into the dining room, sixteen English pairs of eyes turned to look at us. Given the age and charm of the hotel, it felt as if we had stepped into an Agatha Christie murder. We were suddenly two new clues and we might have key information about the murder. But we don't know yet if the murder has yet been committed. I suspect it was done by the man who plays the xylophone and the murder instrument was one of his sticks, the motive relates to a colonial atrocity that destroyed a whole Burmese dynasty, whose final descendent is now the barman in the Strand. He has sent a message to the British Agatha Christie society anonymously suggesting they visit at the time of the full moon (on Wednesday), when a new mystery will be resolved. We will be eating in the hotel for dinner on Wednesday evening. There is someone in the lobby playing a Burmese wooden xylophone and another instrument from time to time. The staff tell us there is wifi and it looks as if there is something but either through government interference or the usual IT demons I have not made a connection.

We met an eighty-two-year-old Burmese Indian woman, Ethel with blue eyes smoking a cheroot, who was the daughter of an English telegraph operator. She is now a tourist guide and told us about her father and the war with the Japanese. She talked about the current government and how things are getting better.

The women and children paint their faces with a liquid cream-coloured powder which stays on the skin. This is both a cosmetic and a way of keeping themselves cool. They look like the bushmen of the Kalahari getting ready to do an exotic dance.

Most of the men wear a form of sarong tied around their middle with a polo shirt or a formal shirt. It looks great as a costume. The women mainly wear pretty sarongs and look fantastic.

There are many monks, young and old, on the street. They wear a deep plum-coloured robe which hangs in abundant and rich folds around their shoulders, quite unlike Thai monks. There are also monk children with shaved heads, small young boys dressed in the dark plum-coloured monk costume.

The country has three-pin plugs like the UK and the electrical plugs fit in without an adapter.

The old city hall has been renovated and now has a new city mayor. It is situated next to a building which was once the largest department stores in Asia. The latter is now closed and is being refurbished.

The streets are filled with people selling goods of all sorts to passers-by. It was interesting to see many English book titles for sale on the street alongside books in Burmese. It seems the English language books are all pirated copies of English text books.

While we have no problem making our way around the city and understanding and being understood English is minimal.

The roundabout at the centre of the town contains a gold painted stupa and pagoda. This is not an elegant or refined monument, like the sacred buildings in Bangkok, but it was full of ordinary people making offerings to their gods. This place is solely for prayers and rituals. Monks do not live on this pagoda. Around the edge of the base of this huge traffic island which is the stupa, there are small shops and stalls which are internet shops, shops selling lottery tickets and other small things.

All city streets have food stalls with women and men cooking food to be eaten at street side. One form of street eating involves various forms of pork cooked in a central pot of stock. It looks very good. There are also market barrows piled high with glace or preserved fruit, lemons, mangos, cherries, plums etc. marinaded in a think molasses-like substance. The fruits taste very good.

We came across people selling tiny tangerines, avocados, grapes, green vegetables

The city has a pagoda, an Anglican cathedral, a Baptist church, a Catholic church, a synagogue and a mosque at least.

Lazy Traveller Blog 6

March 6th 2012, Yangon, Myanmar, staying at Strand Hotel

Yesterday's note was written when I was very tired. I could hardly keep my eyes open. I had not slept the night before and we had travelled to Yangon early in the morning. By the time I sat down to write up a few notes I was feeling very tired. It was hard to remain focused on writing. Today I am feeling far better. I hope I am able to write with a little more feeling and pleasure than yesterday.

Cornelia had arrived in the bar and had already ordered cocktails when I joined her. She has a mission to spread the good news about the wonders of the Gimlet to the good people of Myanmar. She is teaching each cocktail waiter we meet to make the perfect gimlet, viz one part vodka, one part lime, one part sugar syrup (but double strength), shaken and served in a martini glass. I tried it but found it a bit too sweet. I am landing on lime juice and tonic water as a great thirst quencher. Cocktail

43

waiters are a merry bunch of people always keen to learn and experiment and even have another go if their first attempt at a new drink does not work. We had dinner in the Strand Hotel and headed back to our room pretty early. I disappeared at 9pm and did not get up until around 0900 this morning. I felt far better. The terrible tiredness of jetlag had moved on. My dreams were very strange combining ideas from the wars of the roses and my own life. Strange and surreal. After a few hours of such dreams I was happy to wake up and find myself in Yangon again.

The Columbans had a mission to Burma and there was a parlour in Dalgan at the front of the college filled with treasures from Burma. This has been an imaginary place for a long time. It is strange now to be here. Yesterday everything was unexpected and strange. It was strange for the reality of Yangon to be so strong and powerful and so completely different from anything in my imagination filled with objects from Dalgan and images from movies and stories. The reality was more complex, hotter, richer, more demanding and yet at another level even more intriguing and more connected and complex than any image. It was interesting to fly from Bangkok to Yangon and so make the connections between Thailand and Burma. It felt as if Thailand was the richer country, much more at home with both the modern world and its past than Burma which feels like a country unclear about its role in the modern world and yet deeply embedded in cultural heritages linking both India and Thailand. If the country has not been to sleep for the last thirty years like Rip Van Winkle it has been dozing heavily, perhaps also suffering from some form of jetlag.

Today we headed off to the main site in Yangon which is the Shwedagon Paya, a large golden stupa temple complex on the north side of the city. We found a taxi after breakfast and got there around 1030 and left around 1300. We arrived at a strange entrance which has a lift for foreigners, because foreigners are not able to climb the ordinary steps like the other pilgrims. I think it would be good to walk up the long, covered steps and ascend the steps as a pilgrim under the covered walkway. This is constructed in a Thai or Chinese style, with elegant green roofs and golden details.

At the top the staircase opens out into a huge area, on the top of the hill, which is the stupa complex. The complex is built around the large gold encrusted stupa. This is vast monument, which looked like the one we visited yesterday in the centre of the town and the one I also saw at the Thai Royal Palace but this one is very large and the builders created variation and interest in this one by adding, inverting and replicating different layers and building these layers on top of one another, in a way similar to a big Mac. There is a great sense of harmony and unity in the whole stupa but it is a very simple basic structure. The square base and many of the terraces above the base are filled with Buddhas, each in their own niche. The stupa contains multiple images of the Buddha pointing in the four cardinal directions of the compass.

This is a living place of pilgrimage and worship. It is not a monument like the Thai Royal Palace or Wat Phrao. It is filled with ordinary worshippers and pilgrims. It is the largest focus of pilgrimage in Burma/Myanmar and, as in Islam, adults ideally want to visit this place once in their lives. It is a special and personally empowering act to choose to come to this place. People come to be spiritually nourished, to share time with their friends and family and to make offerings to the god, to plead for happiness, well-being and peace for themselves, for their communities and the world. The temple is 2006 years old and the Festival to celebrate this amazing anniversary will culminate with the full moon, tomorrow evening (presumably the Buddhist calendar is based on the moon). We have arrived at the right time. This festival will last fifteen days and during this period particularly beneficial and powerful sutras have been recited by monks on a continuous base and transmitted across the whole complex via loudspeakers. We were hit by these prayers as you enter the temple complex and toward the end of our visit we visited the place where the monk on duty was reciting the sutra. This sutra becomes the mantra that is being repeated during the whole of the visit and is designed to touch our hearts and bring about the blessings it asks for since these words are beneficial and powerful.

This is a place designed to appeal to the senses and involve worshippers and pilgrims in specific activities which become meaningful because of the value and intent the pilgrim brings with him to turn this from an act of tourism into an act of worship. There are beautiful bells in pairs placed all around the complex which are to be hit by worshippers ceremonially. These bell sounds resound beautifully and majestically around the temple.

The complex is full of Buddha statues in various hieratic and static poses including figures of the reclining Buddha. The statues are housed within temple like niches painted white with gold roofs or in large and small halls covered in gold or mirrors. Everything is designed for splendour, to be attractive, to dazzle and daze. This is a building designed to inspire and evoke feelings of amazement and awe in the visitor. It has positive and enriching designs on the pilgrim. The monks and guides have almanacs which identify the day of the week each pilgrim was born and each day of the week has a designated animal. Cornelia was born on

Wednesday and so her animal was an elephant. I was born on Monday so I was a tiger. On eight spots around the base of the stupa there is a place for a worshipper to participate by bathing in water a statue of the Buddha and a statue of the astrological animal for his day of the week. The worshipper scoops water in a silver coloured goblet and bathes the small jade statue of the Buddha five times and then bathes the presiding gold statue behind the Buddha and then bathes the electric lamp post behind the gold deity and finally bathes the figure of the appropriate animal which resides below the Buddha and the water container. We all did it and it was great fun. It was very hot and Buddhas like to be bathed in beautiful cool and refreshing water, as we do. While performing this ritual the worshipper makes a wish which is going to come through. It is a good moment, at the heart of most pilgrimage, to become clear of the wish deep inside one's heart, articulating what it is we most wish for others and for ourselves, clarifying what it is that is troubling us and how that situation could be remedied.

We found a guide, called Miss Kin, who showed us around the complex and explained various things for us. She took us into a number of the halls and one was filled with large terracotta pots laid out on a long table. On each water pot was written a phrase and saying of the Buddha. The worshipper collects two small tin drinking cans from the top of the table and processes around the pots clockwise. The pilgrim collects a small drop from each water pot and so ordinary water becomes holy water, as it is now imbued with the rich and holy sayings and words of the Buddha. At the end you can either drink the water, which was very tempting (this would-be life-giving water imbued with the refreshing and life enhancing

47

words of the Buddha), or you can use it to bathe your arms or head and so the body can take in these refreshing words.

The temple is full of gold and jewels. The stupa is covered with gold leaf and the metal construction hanging from the top of the stupa contains not just bells which sound in the wind, but a vast array of Burmese rubies, other jewels and diamonds. At the centre of this dazzling structure which hangs from the banana bud part of the stupa, above or below the vane, in the form of a garuda (winged dragon or winged lion?), lies a vast and huge diamond. Our guide had pictures of this structure and pictures of the diamond but none of this is visible at ground level.

The large worship halls have many images of the Buddha, usually laid out along the back wall in various configurations. The larger images have neon lights as haloes which are flashing in multiple colours. This was a huge surprise. Blackpool illuminations and Las Vegas have arrived in Yangon. These flashing and radiating lights create a jarring and vulgar note in the midst of all this calm serenity but these temples have always been keen to provide strong sensations to people and worshippers. In each of the large halls there is a large flat TV screen which is broadcasting live images from the red ruby Buddha which is the main idol in the shrine. This Buddha is a small seated fat Buddha with rubies for eyes. Only men are allowed into the sacred area to see the shrine directly but everyone can see the idol and be seen by it via tv. Live tv images of a Buddha statue is even more fascinating than the tv pictures in Saudi of the hajj with the pilgrims walking up and down the covered corridor in Mecca and Medina.

Worshippers are meant to walk around the temple clockwise but there is no set number of times to walk around the complex, as in Mecca and no specific rituals are outlined for pilgrims. Most people come in groups and they come together in the prayer halls and sit down for a picnic together and take photos, while they open their tiffin cans and eat together.

Official photographers wander around the complex ready to take photographs of groups to commemorate their visit to this special place.

This is not a temple. The monks and nuns do not live in the complex. They live outside in convents and monasteries. They come to visit the stupa and to worship and to learn to meditate. One monk we met from India had come to live in Yangon for four years and learn how to meditate. He had been to Birmingham for a visit and he was keen to tell me about the special monk visa he had which allowed him to visit the beautiful city of Birmingham. Monks seem to find an empty niche. They become available for discussion with pilgrims

Groups of Buddhist nuns in pink with shaved heads walk around; the last one has a draped piece of gold cloth over her head. They are very beautiful and very charming.

Lazy Traveller Blog 7

7th March 2012, Yangon, Myanmar, at the airport in Yangon waiting for our flight to Mandalay.

We had a 0400 start, sadly, to be here at the airport for a flight which will leave at 0630. The good news is that we will be in our new hotel by 0900 and ready to rest for the day. Cornelia woke up feeling very unwell and so this journey from hotel to airport and now hanging around in the departure terminal area is a bit fraught with tension. When we get to Mandalay I think we are there for four days. Let's hope that will be enough time for Cornelia to recover and become well again.

We have had a busy few days in Yangon and we will come back here at the end of our stay in Myanmar.

The night before we were both feeling well and went to the Governor's Residence for dinner. It was hard to get there. The concierge had to go through three taxi drivers before we found one who knew where the hotel was. It can't be well known yet. Our concierge could not advise the taxi drivers how to find the hotel. Taxi driver did not know where it was. And later on we had to wait for a taxi to come to the hotel which would drive us back. The Governor's Residence sounds as if it should be an old hotel or an old house but it seems to be a resort hotel similar to those in Indonesia, Malaysia and Bali with a large main wooden structure and rooms around courtyards with water and pools. There was a drama with payment because they would only accept dollars and no credit cards. I had an interesting very large bowl of soup with lemon grass and fish, quite different from Thai soup. It came with interesting condiments that had to be loaded into the steaming broth. It was delicious. The main course was a curry with duck and pickled tea leaves. These tea leaves are a Burmese speciality and I was looking forward to trying them but they were so mild that I did not pick up a new taste in the curry. The steamed vegetables were amusing because they were hard and chewy. This is the hotel where we will stay at the end of the tour.

Yesterday was a major Buddhist public holiday celebrating the full moon, and this moon commemorates the day when the Buddha was convinced by his family to return from the forest and deliver his conclusions about the nature of life, desire, suffering and enlightenment, the great truths. We were going to spend the afternoon visiting the National Museum but it was closed. We were out in the morning visiting Buddhist monuments and in the afternoon we crossed by ferry across the river and wandered on the far side of the river. This is a local village area and very different from the city on the near side of the river. The public holiday also explained why the stalls in Scott Market were closing so decisively the evening before when we had gone to investigate.

Madame Kin came to collect us from the hotel around 0830. We had asked her to guide us for the morning and take us to see some other Buddhist monuments around the city. We headed off first to see the Reclining Buddha, a huge statue, perhaps twice the size of the one in Bangkok but this one had been built in a huge corrugated iron shed, and had lots if mirrors on each pillar and many coloured lights on the railing which surrounded and protected the Buddha. It was a fascinating trip. On the way to this Buddha we saw the monks heading out of the monastery to go begging for food to be served later in the morning. They were heading off with their offering bowls. Later we saw them returning to the monastery.

Mme Kin told us that if the eyes of the Buddha were closed this was a statue of Buddha preparing to die, whereas if he has his eyes open he is resting and relaxing. This Buddha's eyes were open. While the Bangkok reclining giant was restrained and severe, in black and gold, the Yangon Recliner was popular and gaudy with white skin, bright red lips, pink nails and blue eye shadow. He had a long golden gown and the edges of the gown were encrusted with glittering jewels. The Buddha had been financed by a man who was also honoured by the British. We walked to the end of the Buddha and looked at his feet. The names of the Buddha as symbols were inscribed in gold on red onto the Buddha's feet so that the pilgrim could meditate on the nature of his revelation. I had not realised the Buddha had multiple names which were used for meditation, in the same way that Allah has a hundred names and the Virgin's names are contained in the Litany of the Blessed Virgin Mary. The size and gaudiness of the Buddha, his sacred names on his feet, the elegant black haired golden Buddhas these were all surprising.

We collected our shoes and wandered off to a monastery with monks and a large seated Buddha. We had asked Mme Kin to take us to a monastery. The monks eat in silence twice a day, at 0530 and 1130. The abbot and older monks sat at one end of the room, tiny monks at the other end. We asked to visit the monastery but it felt very strange.

Her understanding was not that good and she took us to mean that we wanted to see the monks eat. She had discussed with the monastery the time when the monks ate and we were there.

We had not visited a Burmese monastery. It was a shock that it was a muddy grimy place. This was a training place with sixty to seventy young monks. The students were learning the texts. They had been out begging for food in the morning. They were returning, then washing their robes and their bodies before they were summoned to the hall to eat, the monks sat on the floor around small tables. Some food had been laid out. When they arrived, they came with the food they had collected from donors in the large pots. They sat cross-legged on the floor and ate silently together. The teachers and abbot sat at one of the large room and then the monks sat in order of age, ending at the far end of the room with very young boys sitting at a table.

Before the meal some younger monks were learning to chat and then someone started to hit a wooden gong to call them to eat. However, he wild dogs who lived in the monastery and we had seen laid out in the sunshine woke up at that point and started howling summoning the monks to food because the dogs eat the leftovers from the monks. This chorus of wild dogs was quite amazing. There may have been ten dogs howling away for a while. I did not expect to film wild dogs but they made the most amazing noise.

This was a poor monastery. It had few buildings and the buildings were quite derelict and yet, despite all this, the monks looked elegant in their dark plum-coloured robes and strong colours, shaved heads and kind smiles.

The sitting Buddha and the viewing hall were not a surprise, but the monks and the wild dogs were a big surprise and inspired awe in one case (the monks) and surreal amusement in the other case (the dogs)

Mme Kin explained she was a tour guide in Japanese, Spanish and English. Her English understanding was not very good but she had taught Japanese to the Burmese for thirty years. Her son had gone to Japan to study business because his Japanese was good because of his mother. He did well, graduated, found a job in Japan and found a wife. He had no interest in coming back to Myanmar. And so Mme Kin was sad. He was their only child. Mme Kin showed us photos of her son very proudly. There was a strange graduation photograph on pedestals like Olympic game, son on highest pedestals and parents on two lower pedestals, whole family looking amazing and very happy. Her husband had worked in Malaysia for ten years or so. We were the same age!

Back to the hotel for lime tonics and then off to ferry to cross the Yangon river. The ferry just goes back and forth across the river, bringing people from the city into the country and back. The ferry was packed. There were some benches and then lots of seats from an infant school in bright green and pink plastic. The monks sat quietly at one of the boat. Yung boys were walking around with trays on their heads selling sweets, another lady was selling cooked chicken and birds' eggs, other boys were selling food to attract seagulls. A rickshaw driver talked to us persistently in fairly good English and told us about bad his luck was at the moment.

A father and his sons were selling bleach, detergent and stain remover. Amazing patter and then walked around selling goods. We walked around the village and then stopped to admire the bread maker movies. The ferry and the bread maker were great surprises.

Further along Strand road was another stupa I visited on my own, Botataung Paya—an old monk started to talk to me, he had the most amazing long hair coming out of his ears and incredible eyebrows. I have never seen such long hair sprouting from someone's ears and eyebrows. He had been chewing betel nuts for his whole life and so his teeth had worn down to black stumps and his mouth was black. It was hard to look at him he was so strange and disturbing. He was far worse than the hairy and bearded Rowan Williams. He was keen to talk to me at length about the political situation in Myanmar politics. He talked about the UN trilateral commission which wanted to interfere in the internal governance of Myanmar. He favoured a solution like the one in East Timor where ASEAN forces went in but then left and the liberation of Poland which involved no foreign or UN troops. He was concerned that Myanmar's liberation did not involve UN troops because he argued the UN never leave. He did not think Aung San Sui Kyi will be able to exercise any power if she wins the election on 1st April. Mme Kin was also worried about what was going to happen after the election. The monk was afraid that the West will do the wrong thing. The message was leave us alone and leave us to our own affairs. Don't interfere in the internal politics of Myanmar. The monk helped our hope that Aung San Sui Kyi would wait for the General Election in few years (2015?) and then she might be able to exercise some power. He was worried that since her son was in the UK the US and UK were holding her to ransom. I found it hard to follow the argument, to listen and to look at this disturbing old man. I suppose he was a nasty and disturbing surprise.

The tourist information at this stupa was very anti British and had lots of discussion about how the British had ransacked the cultural treasures of this temple and Myanmar.

Three young women came up to the monk and pressed money into his hands and wanted his blessing. He changed his pose and accepted their bows, adoration and their offering., He wanted me to make a donation. If he had asked me anything and did not talk the whole thirty minutes he may have got a donation. But by that stage I was keen to get away.

The stupa which had been rebuilt in the twentieth century with cement was empty but the style of building was still not able to construct a dome from the inside of the stupa. Instead the inside had been hollowed out, covered in gold leaf and then the gold leaf was protected with glass panels. The roof was supported by huge pillars. At the centre of the stupa was a reliquary with some of the hairs of the Buddha given to two Burmese merchants who were visiting India where Buddha was enlightened forty-nine days after his enlightenment. Because Buddha knew that Burma was going to become a stronghold of Buddhism, the story went, he gave the merchants eight hairs to bring back with them. The others were dispersed around the country and two remained in this stupa.

The monk was a surprise, not a very pleasant one. I was pleased to get away and walk back to the hotel along the Strand Road, passing by young men playing football very skilfully in their bare feet. Football is an international culture.

We headed back around sundown to the Shwedagon Paya to see what happened at this major festival. As the sun set, neon lights were switched on. The place was filled with thousands of people, milling around, waiting in queues for something, walking around with each other. It was a warm and gentle atmosphere. Each niche with its Buddha was decorated with lights and the large viewing halls were lit in a variety of zany ways. It was a magical and rather simple effect. The space was packed with people coming to make their worship on this special evening with their families. The lights were colourful, they flashed and moved furiously, in sunburst or in syncopated rhythms as if each set of lights was competing with the others. We were told that donors had to propose a lighting plan and these were reviewed and approved by the trustees of the site. These amazing lights were a bright and mysterious response to this special full moon at this stage of the year. The whole stupa complex was full of people wandering around, sitting on the floor worshipping towards the stupa or towards an image of the Buddha and full of warm family feeling. This part of Yangon had become a strange amalgam of Las Vegas, Blackpool and competed with the wild neon displays on Shanghai's Nanjing Road. These sort of effects we don't associate with religion because they seem too popular, garish and unrestrained, but none of these considerations were at work here. Everyone was happily enjoying the lights while focusing showing their gratitude to Buddha and asking for more good things in the year to come.

While we were taking pictures in one of the pavilions and waiting for something to happen around 1900, a mother started to talk to us in English. She told us about the festival, the lights, the season and what this festival meant in Buddhism. We then met her husband, her son and her adopted daughter and we heard more about the family. It was a lovely moment and a complete surprise. We had attempted to speak to a number of the worshippers but they were embarrassed and not keen to get involved.

This is the day Buddha was encouraged to come back to his family from the forest and tell those he had left behind the four great lessons he had learnt about suffering, desire and enlightenment.

We headed down by the foreigners' elevator and then found a taxi to drive us back to the Strand hotel for dinner and departure for Mandalay early this morning.

Lazy Traveller Blog 8

8th March 2012, Hotel by Red Canal, Mandalay

Cornelia woke up ill this morning and was projectile vomiting by the time we got out of the car at the airport. She was in an unsteady state at the airport and by the time we took off around 0630 she was a ghostly shade of very pale white. We arrived in Mandalay around 0830 with a touch down in Bagan (I think). It is a constant surprise how fragile our bodies are. We can seem to be going at full belt, able to tackle anything and everything and then within a few minutes our world has changed and we find ourselves incapable of remaining upright and our bodies are in meltdown. Why do these things seem more likely to happen when we are on vacation? We found that the new airport in Mandalay is fifty kilometers out of the town and it took us a long time to get into the city. By the time we arrived Cornelia had changed from white back to flesh colour.

It was fascinating to fly over the country this morning. It was dry and flat except along the vast river systems when the land turned green and seemed to be full of paddy fields.

We were talking about emerging markets over the last few days and Cornelia told me that the latest thing is not emerging markets but frontier markets where the potential for gain is even greater than in an emerging market but where the risks are even higher. If Bangkok is an emerging market Myanmar is a frontier market and the sticky edge of the frontier seems to be Mandalay. This is a frontier city. Mandalay is a frontier town and tourism here is decidedly edgy.

Hotels seemed to be divided into army or military hotels: the latter seem large and well equipped but ideologically unsound while the non-military hotels or guesthouses which may be ideologically sound but stretch the imagination as well as the wallet.

It is rare surprise to visit a country which has so many hang ups and contorted rituals about cash and money. Some people insist on being paid in dollars, others only in local currency. Hotels refuse to take credit cards except with a surcharge of 15% in certain cases. In these cases they arrange for the credit card to be processed by a Las Vegas hotel. Curiouser and curiouser. The official tourist bureau I tried to use today to cash a cheque would not give me a receipt and offered a rate of 780 to the dollar whereas the rate at the airport currency counter when we arrived was 810. I went in search of a few banks in Mandalay but they would not exchange foreign currency and sent me onto another small place in an obscure part of town which was official. The young people at this office were very pleasant and spent a long time checking my passport and the quality of the bank note and gave me a rate of 815 to the dollar, a receipt and a pleasant experience. Dollar notes, in certain cases, have to be in high denominations, in others only small denominations are acceptable. We are told that the exit tax has to be paid in new $10 bills. These rules and regulations seem designed to drive mad foreigners even madder. No taxi is metered and there is always a special price for foreigners because the locals are so poor. It is like a Humpty Dumpty Land where words mean whatever you want them to mean and money, lack of it or too much of it, is a major issue.

Perhaps this is normal. I remember when I first arrived in China I was very confused and quite lost and then I met an old American couple, Tom and Mary, who had just arrived in Shanghai after teaching for five years in the middle of the country. They saw everything in Nanhui, where we were living on the outskirts of Shanghai, in a very good and positive light and I fell in quickly with their view of the world. They taught me to love China. They were the enlightened version of Baucis and Philemon who ended up in China rather than on the top of a mountain.

The city of Mandalay is built around a large old fort on a grid pattern. There is a large closed market area in the centre of the town with a British-style clock tower and an imperial railway station. It is as if the British built or adapted the outlines of a city but then something happened and all has returned to the wild. And the wild is not the attractive wild of a cute primitivism but the dark and bitter wild of a poor and derelict city.

To the north east of the fort lies few things to see and Mandalay Hill which is a high point overlooking the city. Along some of the city streets there are the tired and ruined remains of Christian churches of many Christian persuasions, the monument to brave souls (Lear-like figures of passionate intensity), men and women who came here in an earlier time and tried to leave some impact on a city in terms of Christian buildings they were unable to come to terms with. These places now lie derelict even when there are a few guardians hanging around.

In hotel terms frontier as opposed to emerging means a room in Mandalay one quarter of the size for the same price as the vast room we had in Yangon. We have moved from an old traditional hotel in the centre of Yangon across from the ferry to a small boutique hotel with a pool with minuscule rooms but very friendly staff. It was a surprise to be greeted so warmly by the staff but this hotel is even more of an enclave from the surrounding city than the Strand in Yangon.

Cornelia went to bed as soon as we arrived and I headed into town to exchange some currency. The streets are wild, dirty and full of hard-nosed enterprise. The heat is intense. I can imagine the empire builders arriving here and being as overwhelmed as we are by everything.

The celebration last night in Yangon commemorates the Buddha's understanding of the harsh nature of existence and what it is going to be required to come to terms with this reality. The Buddha had to give up all illusions he had about man and nature before he could come to his truths and what he left was his teaching which others turned into a set of rituals and practices to keep these truths alive. Today I was thinking of poor foolish and stupid King Lear cast out onto the moor, as I was walking around Mandalay. Lear, like the Buddha, has to lose all illusions about himself and the world around him and come to terms with the brute facts of nature and the foolishness of his own soul. Shakespeare shows us Lear suffering as he loses his illusions and goes quietly mad in the face of reality. Lear leaves no teachings. Shakespeare leaves Lear and shows us the nature of man. The Buddha does not show us the nature of his own suffering. He attempts to overcome it in his teachings. Perhaps Buddha is the wiser but I favour Lear and Shakespeare. Myanmar is a poor country which must have suffered mismanagement for decades. The poverty here is far worse than most of what I met in China. It is hard to see what happened and why things are as bad as they are. It is hard to see a country in such a rank state. I am not sure that it is good to be a tourist here. It is not just that it is patronising and inappropriate to watch the spectacle of this poverty but it seems naïve and fatuous to extract from it some cultural enlightenment.

We go on travels to be enlightened, energised, reempowered, and revitalised. We come to find some new power within ourselves by being in contact with some external power, the exotic, the other, the warm, the cultural heritage of the wisdom of others. We are as naïve as poor Lear and we quickly learn to our cost that we are on the moor with Lear, not at all where we thought we were going to be in a luxury hotel firmly ensconced in the safety of western luxury.

It seems strange that as travellers we start off on the upper edge of the Maslow scale, a bit like Lear when he is disposing of his kingdom to his three daughters and agreeing the terms of his retirement, but quickly, like Lear, we plunge down the Maslow scale to end up in a state of bare survival.

Lazy Traveller Blog 9

9th March 2012, Hotel by the Red Canal, Mandalay

We had a good day sight-seeing in Mandalay with a driver who joined us at lunch time. Cornelia had a good night and we were both able to eat breakfast. The staff are very friendly and they are keen to practice their English. Each evening there is a cocktail session from 1800-1900 and the staff serve cocktails and nibbles. The rooms at this hotel are very small—dinky even by UK standards and very small for Myanmar so the hotel has decided to focus on very friendly and delightful staff and cocktail hours. These times each day are great opportunities to hear what other people are doing and what they are making of their time in Myanmar. Tonight I was talking to a couple from Newcastle who are having the time of their lives. They have given me the name of their guide in Bagan who may be able to help us when we get there in a few days. Cornelia was chatting to a couple from Wimbledon who had been to see a British hill station and spent time in the botanical gardens. They did not get on well with one another.

But today since we were both well we set out to explore Mandalay and be surprised at what we found.

First of all we went to investigate the Mandalay Fort and Palace which dominates the centre of Mandalay. The city was created on a grid pattern around the fort by one of the last kings of Burma who moved the capital to Mandalay where it was the capital for about twenty years before the British overthrew the king and sent him into exile in India. Most of the palace was destroyed by Japanese bombs during the war and in the last twenty years it was rebuilt using forced labour and concrete rather than wood and all the palace buildings have corrugated red iron roofs and white look out towers.

It was fascinating to walk through the Eastern fort gate (the only one foreigners are allowed to use) and walk along what is now an army encampment but was originally the royal outer palace. It felt as if the model for the palace was the great imperial palaces of China, which themselves are built as royal temples with multiple audience halls, each following the other. In the temples each hall has one or more different forms of the Buddha (one looking west and the other looking east). In the Forbidden City each hall was used for a particular imperial ritual. In the case of this palace there should have been a series of halls, each with a different throne and used to conduct different business. At the eastern end of the complex there were two pavilions one on each side and at the western end of the palace there was a Queen's audience hall which is now used as cultural museum. It was a sad and derelict place, situated in an amazing and magnificent park. It was a folly created by a king who had a very short time to reign before he was murdered in this palace he had built to establish a new reign and a new era for Burma with its capital in Mandalay. It turned out to be a folly. It is as if the religious structures in Myanmar have survived whereas all other forms of civilian life are transitory and do not abide. Walking around this palace was like entering the world of Ozymandias. It was fascinating and disturbing. In certain halls there was a throne and wax figures of the king and his wife. These made a very sad impression and seemed meaningless.

It is hard to identify in my mind what I meant by Burma. When I arrived in Kyoto having lived in Tokyo for a while I realised that Kyoto was what I expected from Japan. Tokyo was a compete and disturbing surprise. Kyoto recalled childhood images of Japan. But what do I mean by Burma? I recall certain Burmese artefacts from Dalgan and there is an exotic mystery inherent in certain names such as Rangoon, Mandalay and the Irawaddy but what are the images behind these words? I am not sure. I think I have confused Burma and Siam and both are wrapped up in the splendour of the King and I. The Royal Palace, when it was vibrant and full of life may have been all that we mean by the once former glory of Burma but now it is a sad, red corrugated roofed shell.

Later in the afternoon, however, we visited the Shwenandaw Kyaung not far from the hotel. This was a good surprise. It was the royal apartment which King Mindon had built for himself as the centrepiece of his new palace. It was a splendid wooden structure built on stone plinths and featured enormously elaborate wooden carvings which had all been once gilded. The central chamber was still gilded and there was some gilding on some of the outer panels which had not been subject to heavy weather. King Mindon had been murdered by his wife or brother in this room and the new king decided he could not use this apartment in the palace he had inherited from the murdered king so he had it transported to the current location and gave it to the monks who converted it from a royal apartment into a Buddhist audience hall. Because it was beyond the royal fortress it was not bombed by the Japanese and survived. This was one of the two very fine buildings we saw today.

A lot of the other religious buildings we visited were built after the palace was built in 1850 and they were designed to turn Mandalay into a religious centre of pilgrimage. Two of the temples featured the Buddhist scriptures written onto stone tablets, each tablet or memorial stone encased in a shrine niche, as we saw in Yangon. In one temple there were more than seven hundred of these white-painted niches, each niche was identical and each contained a stone tablet with the Buddha's words. These niches were all lined up in multiple rows and straight lines radiating around a central golden stupa. The decoration of the central temple and the corridors leading from one quarter to the next featured very bright garish colours and simple mirrors and coloured lights to enhance the overall spectacle and to appeal. These structures were clearly designed to attract large numbers of pilgrims but unlike the vast structure and sula (pagoda) in Yangon these temples now do not have pilgrims nor monks. They were empty today except for a few foreign tourists and a few very keen girls keen to sell postcards or wind chimes. This was like a ghost city, a city which had been built with structures, such as the palace and these Buddhist monuments, designed to attract and dazzle many people but everything had changed, a bubble had burst, an illusion collapsed and all that was left were monuments without much life. Monuments need people and attention if they are to retain some vitality and meaning.

However, on the western edge of the city, down a dirt track we visited a superb monastery, the best we have visited so far, built of wood, with very beautiful carving on every surface, with each door containing musician figures. The Shwe in Bin Kyaung was built at the same time as the Palace by two Chinese merchant brothers as a monastery. It was a beautiful place. It was not gilded like the earlier royal apartment but the carving may have been done by the same people. this was an elongated structure set on high stone stilts. At one end there was a huge carved and gilded pagoda like tower, similar to a steeple. In the middle there was the dark and high mysterious audience chamber with the images of the Buddha. This was a beautiful space. The shutters along one side of the hall had been raised to let in light. It was a light and airy space, a place out of a fairy tale or an exotic old story of Burma. At the far end of the audience chamber were two glass cabinets filled with gold-edged books which were clearly treasures of this monastery. The monks lived in pavilions around the chapel and below the chapel on ground level was a deep well.

This was a quiet and compelling place and was a wonderful surprise, whereas our visit to Mandalay Hill was disturbing for all the wrong reasons. The Hill looms over the palace and fort and was meant to be visited by Buddha when he was a chicken. The palace was built close to the Hill to take advantage of the power this hill accrued because of its religious connection. We got to the top by way of an escalator. All the halls and areas at the top of the hill were very dirty and outside the main audience chamber there were many photos of military leaders worshipping at the shrine. These are the first signs of any military presence we have seen. There are no soldiers on the streets or at the airports. There are no visible signs of the military rulers. We have not seen large expensive cars rushing past carrying officers. We have not seen many large army buildings. Even the fort which is now an army barracks had only a few guards at the gates but no heavy presence. Madame Kin told us that there is an agreement that soldiers don't appear on the streets. This seems correct. But it was as if these photographs at this shrine were evidence of a strange concordat between the military rulers and the Buddhist leaders, each power validating the other in some unholy and tenuous alliance. It felt strange. We were at the top of the hill when it was very smoggy and we could not even see the fortress and palace below. This summit is meant to be an ideal place for sunset but not at this time of the year. The monuments were neglected and the audience chambers had officious guardians. It was surprisingly creepy but we did our duty and visited it.

We ended up at a hotel on the west bank of the Irawaddy with a rooftop bar and restaurant. We watched as the sun started to go down over this huge and amazing river. This was a wonderful natural spectacle, the first time we have seen the Irawaddy from the ground. It is a vast river like the Huang Pu in Shanghai, on which the city was founded and clearly a main artery up and down country. This was a wonderful position from which to view the river and to look out to Mingun a place on the far side of the river we have not been able to visit.

We sat on the rooftop drinking a local Myanmar beer and read about George Orwell and Rudyard Kipling and their time in Burma.

On the way back to the hotel we stopped off at a gold-beating factory which showed us how gold leaf is made by hand. Tomorrow we will see people gilding the Buddha in a temple outside the city. And we visited a new shopping mall on five floors, opened by Korean entrepreneurs and completely unlike anything else in Mandalay. This is the future. It was fascinating to see who was in this shopping mall, what was being sold and how the people were coping with this strange new experience of abundance which could not be more different from the scarcity and poverty visible everywhere else in the city.

We also started to read more about Burmese history and learnt that the British brought most of the Indians to Burma to manage the country on their behalf. It did not work and the Indians and the British were fiercely resented. The Buddhist monks and the monasteries, not the king, seemed to have the real power in the country. Buddhism is a strong and long-lasting institution. And yet the army and the monks seem to be in an uneasy alliance, both believing they represent the best interests of the country and the people.

Tonight the mosquitos are biting and I am covered with white bumps where I have been bitten.

Lazy Traveller Blog 10

10th March 2012

Hotel by the Red Canal,
Visiting towns and area outside Mandalay.

This is a journal about our time yesterday visiting the three ancient cities around Mandalay and the first time we spent in rural Mandalay. However, this morning we are now on the ferry boat which will take us from Mandalay to Bagan. We got up early, had breakfast, checked out and the staff were on hand to say goodbye and get us to the boat on time. We had heard from Norwegian travellers last night that this ferry was going to be rough, with too few seats and we needed strong cushions. But nevertheless we got to the ferry with plenty of time, found seats looking out across the Irawaddy and the seats are not too bad. We should be on the ferry for about seven or eight hours. It is likely to be a great way of seeing new parts of Myanmar and getting a sense of life lived along the riverbank (shades of *Tales of the Riverbank* and *Wind in the Willows*).

At this stage I have lost any sense of time and I am no longer sure of the day of the week. We are now occupying a Burmese time bubble and we float from one place to another. I am not reading the Shakespeare poems I had intended to read. But instead I have been reading Lisa Appignanesi's new book, *All About Love*. This is great reading for the end of the day. Yesterday was a busy day. We were in a car moving around from 0830 until around 1700. The heat at this time of the year, by the middle of the morning, is very intense and exhausting. We had no inclination for lunch and it was good to get back in the afternoon for a shower, many drinks and supper.

We were due to visit the three ancient cities of old Burma and see life in rural Mandalay since these old cities have now reverted to rural areas. I have had a bad chest infection since I left the UK and yesterday my cough was getting worse and my energy has been dropping partly caused by a troubled night which nevertheless was filled with sweet dreams. It is hard now to go for such a length of time with so little communication with the outside world. The hotel notionally had email and a broadband connection and I managed to send out a very short note from Gmail saying that we were about to leave Mandalay and all was well but I could not look at Yahoo mail at all and I have not been able to communicate now for about a week. This is rare in this day and age to have a place cut off from the rest of the world in terms of wifi and a broadband connection. In China even in rural areas it was possible to send and receive emails. Myanmar is making it difficult for this sort of normal communication to occur. It is a bad sign for any regime when they are so out of touch that they inhibit communications between citizens and between visitors and the outside world. This failure indicates a real sense of fear, paranoia and wilful isolation.

Our first step yesterday was at Mahamuni Paya. This temple holds a largish contented sitting Buddha. Buddhist men (not women) are allowed to gild the statue with more gold leaf. His body has changed shape but his face has remained human and unchanged. Families in full national costume come to have their photographs taken in front of this image and the helpers of the photographers then appear with huge lights which lighten up the family and the image. The Buddha was interesting but nothing special and the temple was tacky and quite ordinary but what was surprising and delightful at this place was that it was the temple where young people (or perhaps young men) come to be displayed as young men, perhaps. Families came in ceremonial costume with their sons to process around the temple and have ceremonial and special photos taken. The little boys were shielded by parasols carried by attendants like a young prince or a Buddha.

What made these fascinating and wonderful scenes even more amazing was the costume of the young men. These young men in their late teens, accompanied by their younger brothers, also in ceremonial costume and their parents, aunts, uncles, grandparents etc. were dressed very strangely. It was as if they had been made up as young women. They had white face paint, red lips, lots of eye shadow and very feminine dresses and high heels. It was a strange sight because they also had pencil line moustaches in the midst of all this femininity.

On the way into this temple, since I was wearing shorts, I was told by the temple guardians that I should wear one of the local longhi, or sarongs. The lady told me to stand in the middle of the material and she wrapped it around me. I had no sense of what it looked like and how strange it looked but the local people thought it very amusing and a few fellow tourists came up to me with funny comments. I should have had a photo taken.

This was a large temple and perhaps this time of the year is auspicious for these family initiation ceremonies. There were many families at the temple all in great spirits parading around the temple grounds, ready to line up in front of the image of the Buddha to have their special photos taken, just as small children in the west used to have their photos taken annually sitting on Santa's lap.

However, as we left the temple and journeyed on to the next place, for a white stupa moment, we saw even more amazing processions heading towards the temple. In some cases the men were on horses decorated in bright colours and in one case the procession was led by a small elephant carrying a young man dressed like in very female attire.

The large reclining Buddha in Yangong looked very feminine in terms of bright red lips, dark blue eye shadow and pink nails. Perhaps this costume represents old courtly style dress. It was fascinating. The processions on the streets heading to the temple were even more interesting. The horses and elephant were followed by long lines of couples in beautiful traditional dress carrying offerings of lotus blooms and other gifts.

There were few remains of the ancient cities and those remains had been reconstructed in the 19th and 20th centuries. We did not see a lot which went back beyond 1830 or so.

We think we are travelling independently and avoiding the tourist trail. We all realise at some level how contaminated and contaminating is the experience of tourism. But we are fooling ourselves clearly. All the people we meet and see are carrying the same Lonely Planet Guide to Myanmar. We carry these books around like Chairman Mao's *Little Red Book*. And when we ask advice about a driver and what to see in this area we are told exactly what is in the book. We have an illusion of freedom but it is just that, an illusion. The Buddha would laugh and ask us what we expected. The other guests in the hotel and the hotel told us we should see the sight of the monks walking in procession for lunch at a monastery. We ended up Maha Ganayon Kyaung at the right time around 1100.

At 1115 the monks formed a long procession in two lines and walked into the hall where they collected their lunch. But surrounding this simple procession were hordes of unruly and mad tourists from around the world, who had all been told that this was the thing not to miss.

The monks carried off the procession very well. Each carried with him his bowl, a mug and a towel. The very young boys were dressed in white. These are mainly young monks in their late teens and early twenties and this monastery, which is considered strict and has a good abbot, is equivalent to a summer school for Burmese young men, who come here to learn about Buddhism, themselves and spend some time as a monk away from their family. They stay as long as they want to. They have their heads shaved and put on the plum-coloured robes of a monk and they learn to be silent, to meditate, to conduct themselves with dignity and restraint. Each day they have to head off with their yellow bowl to collect food which is offered to them by the local people. they bring this back to the monastery and eat around 1115. We have not seen these monks sing or chant together and we do not see them conducting ceremonies in the monasteries or the shrines. This large institution on the outskirts of Mandalay is a finishing school for young men, equivalent in some way to Swiss young men heading off for national service. The monks processed with great elegance, restraint, grace, although they were being treated like animals in the zoo or a celebrate at a movie premiere. The tourists on the other hand conducted themselves pretty badly, pushing and shoving in case they missed anything. The tourists were hungry for sensation and a good shot. We were living in a world of illusions. Some of the tourists invaded the street where the monks were meant to be walking and the monk guardians had to ask them to step aside. A Korean tourist insisted in walking into the dining hall and taking photos even with her shoes on. This caused scandal and she was asked to leave but she did not.

I had a sense that this procession was now a big tourism spectacle, equivalent to the changing of the guard outside Buckingham Palace, a ritual which has become a colourful and splendid spectacle for tourists. It must have been interesting for the young monks to take on board the experience of becoming such a spectacle and see these foreigners acting like animals.

Burma already has plenty of tourists. We saw many yesterday. I thought there were twenty coach loads. We are tourists too. The procession of monks was a strange and disturbing experience. I remember in China how horrible it was to be stared at again and again for hours when Chinese people were dumb struck to be confronted by a live foreigner for the first time in their lives. We were spectacles, oddities, figures from another world. I hated it.

The second area we investigated yesterday was Amarapura. This was also billed as a former and ancient city but all that remained were hills full of charming golden stupas and pagoda. These structures create an exotic and attractive landscape. There has been religious tourism, or pilgrimage, in this area a long time before contemporary cultural tourism and this religious tourism is well developed. The hills have steps cut into them and covered pathways pilgrims can use to walk up the mountain sides, stopping at different shrines on the way, collecting religious icons and praying to different forms of the Buddha. Now this all looks very commercial. There are local people and the monks walk up and down these paths but I did not get a sense of religious ritual. This place is in transition from a religious to a consumer society.

The Buddha images are the same and this provokes new questions about difference and similarity. We value difference, the particular, the momentary, the passing and evanescent. Our aesthetic sensibility is completely contrary to the Buddha who tells us that transience is about illusion, suffering and pain and to find enlightenment and peace we must remove ourselves from these illusions. The goal for the Buddha is to lose and leave behind the personal and be resolved into the permanent, the passionless, pure knowledge beyond desire and death. But we also know from the west that the ego is a cause of suffering. We realise our emotions are quite mad and our inner world is irrational, chaotic and can give us as much pain as pleasure. We know the will is contaminated and leads to selfishness, naivety, a will to power and self-righteousness. We may not go along with the Buddha's solution although it is clear it worked for this sort of society for many centuries. We are still searching but the Buddha is a fascinating wise man who clearly has much insight into the right questions to ask and the illusions of the ego.

I am still involved in and fascinated by the vagaries and illusions of the ego. These simple smiling statues promising release if I give up everything do not yet appeal to me although I am keen to hear about how to unravel the madness of the ego and find a peace other than by naïve striving. Sadly yesterday's visit to the Buddhist shrines on Amarapura did not give me the direction I might have been looking for. The journey continues.

At one of the largest hill top shrines, Pahtodawgyi, a monk showed us around in cool shades. He opened reliquary gates to show us many Buddhas all lined up in ecstasy, expecting some response from us and then at the end he asked each of us for a dollar. Apparently the monks don't beg for their food each morning and when they are walking around early in the morning with their votive pot they must not look anyone in the eye. They receive the gifts people want to make. It may work I am not sure. I am suspicious as a westerner and my suspicion is the air I breathe. It is a strange experience to be in a place where religious suspicion is not allowed whereas political suspicion is both rife and unspoken. This is a strange humpty dumpty world of wonderland where words mean what people want them to mean and they can change depending on our intentions. Myanmar is marketed as a holiday destination for those who are travellers not tourists but we all follow the same book, almost slavishly, and since there is no infrastructure of educated guides, as there is in Egypt, even the guides follow the same routes and repeat the words in the Lonely Planet guide. We are all living various levels of illusion. The words of Buddha have been replaced by the words of Lonely Planet. How amazing!

In one of the temples the doctrine of Buddha was outlined in English and I stood next to an Italian translating it for his friends. This felt a strange experience. The doctrine made more sense in Myanmar in this hot extreme climate in a land subject to monsoons, earthquakes, revolution and the fall of empires than it does at home. Moods, emotions, pain, romantic desire, happiness and accomplishment are all illusions. We live in a world of our own imagining. We live in a world of our illusions. Only the permanent is true and the permanent is beyond suffering and illusion. Although the people in Myanmar are very charming they don't make a case for Buddhism. Myanmar is not the answer to a question I can formulate. It is both exotic and banal. Obscure and very trivial. Poor and tremendously vibrant. Enticing and repulsive.

For the afternoon we moved from stupa Burma on the hills around the Irawaddy to rural Myanmar and the old capital of Inwe (or Avi). We went the huge river on a small ferry boat and then visited the four monuments by horse and cart. This was a lot of fun. The buildings were fascinating but the life we passed through was far more interesting and this is the nearest we have got to seeing and participating in rural Myanmar, looking at the stilted wooden cabins, watching the beautiful white cows walking along the dirt tracks, with pigs, chickens, dogs and people wandering from cabin to cabin.

Two special monasteries were included on our trip; one built in wood to a traditional style we had seen at its best in Mandalay, there built by Chinese merchants, and the other built in stone to the same design. And we also visited a ruined stupa, a ruined watchtower. The former capital city and a royal palace had been destroyed by an earthquake. The land had returned to subsistence farming and rich green paddy fields. The monasteries were interesting architecturally. The wooden monastery was exquisite and probably the best we have seen, with an octagonal pagoda at one end of the raised platform and the rectangular audience chamber hall at the other with its idol. The secular buildings looked vaguely Indian in style but it was impossible to gain any sense of this lost city and any splendour it may have had.

The surprises were not the buildings however, but the people who constitute the real culture which we don't get close to and remains strange and exotic. As drifting tourists we live in a transitory and strange dream world. We have no understanding of the monks, especially the young monks we see begging and processing for lunch. We have no understanding of the small children at school in the monastery learning to read and write. The ordinary schools are now closed for three months holidays and so the children are out of the streets selling souvenirs on the small ferries. They have some English but the people and their way of life, thinking and their culture is beyond us and remains a mystery.

The day of travelling and sight-seeing ended at the large teak bridge of U Bein — at this stage of the year the river is low and the river plain has mainly become paddy fields and rich green stretches full of vibrant crops. There was a large herd of fat and very happy ducks being herded from one side to another by a figure who was perhaps a duck shepherd. He made a noise and banged a paddle onto the water and the ducks swam towards him. These sights were beautiful. This is our ideal and splendid image of Indochina: this was it and it was inspiring, beautiful and moving. The long bridge was like the Great Wall of China and snaked its way in front of us to the far side where there more golden stupas and pagodas. You can see why the unfolding scroll painting became a visual form in this landscape.

80

People were walking back and forth across the beautiful bridge and enjoying the view and one another. It was a sort of heaven.

Lazy Traveller Blog 11

March 11th 2012, Hotel (very complicated name) in Bagan, called by the British Pagan

This could be a short journal note today. It is late, 2045. We have had dinner at the hotel where we arrived at 1815 and there will be a driver and a tour guide who arrive tomorrow morning at 0800 to show us around Bagan.

Today we left the hotel in Mandalay around 0700 and got onto the boat at the jetty and sailed until 1800. A long day, but it was restful. It was a good opportunity to catch up with yesterday's blog, sleep a little, have lunch and read a lot. We thought we might not be able to get seat but we were on the boat early and we got seats. When we left the temperature was very mild but by 1130 it was very hot and that heat continued as usual until 1430 when it starts to subside. This time of the year, mid-March, is too late to travel in Myanmar. Schools have closed and that is a good indication that this is a season which is too hot to do anything. Yesterday (or the day before) Francesca visited a hill station where the British would retreat to at this time of the year, until the monsoons arrived. She enjoyed her trip.

We were on the boat for a long time. it was a restful journey. We seemed to pull in to the side of the river twice but this was to let staff on and off. At one stage the local people were throwing bananas onto the boat. It felt rather amusing. Were they throwing the bananas at us, like monkeys in the zoo, with us as the monkeys? Or were we the monkeys being entertained by this strange local custom of begging foreigners with the use of bananas? Neither way, it did not seem politically very correct and I noticed many unopened bananas on the boat for the rest of the trip.

I used the time on the boat to catch up with yesterday's blog and to read a lot more from Lisa Appignanesi's book *All About Love*. It was a great read and just what I needed.

We have heard that it is even warmer in Bagan than it was in Mandalay. We have the guide arriving at 0800 so that we can stop around 1400 and give in. it is going to be tough trying to walk around in this fierce heat. I must bring my hat.

I wanted to write today about the people we met at the Red Canal Hotel in Mandalay. The staff were all very charming and sweet, very young, smart and very keen to help us. This was outstanding service and even better than we had in Yangon. The hotel where we are now in Bagan is a splendid resource hotel but the staff are older and less focused. Service is longer and it is all more abstract and impersonal whereas the service at the Red Canal was very personal and charming. The young people looked amazing in their uniforms and they went out of their way to help us.

Yesterday we came back from a trip and Cornelia asked one of the boys to wash her shoes. He came back with them thirty minutes later and she said they were cleaner than when she arrived in Myanmar. He had been talking to me since we arrived and told me he has English lessons with a local monk and he was taught by an Irish lady, Margaret, who came to stay in the monastery for a few years. He has chosen to become a Christian and he was very keen to talk and get my email address. He wanted to talk to me about football and his favourite player is Christian Reynaldo or Ferdinand and he now follows Real Madrid because this is where he plays.

The assistant manager was an Indian Myanmar and was very professional and appeared each evening to ask about how we were getting on.

We were sorry to leave.

We met the other guests each evening at a happy hour from 1800. We met Francesca from Chiasso in the Tessin in Switzerland who was travelling on her own for four weeks in Myanmar. She was a wise old owl and came back each evening with a cold eye on what she had seen during the day. She changed her room twice because the rooms were so small. Last night I talked to two Norwegian couples. They had difficulty speaking English but one husband told me that they spend four months each year in Thailand (October, November, January and February) returning to Stavanger for Christmas. They had done this same trip last year at the end of their time in Thailand and had persuaded another Norwegian couple to join them for this tour this year.

Cornelia was talking to a couple from Wimbledon but they fell out and we did not see them again.

I talked to the Robinsons from Newcastle who were full of admiration for everything they were seeing in Myanmar. They gave me the name of a good guide here in Bagan. I enjoyed talking to them. They told us about the monks' procession and the presentation at the gold Buddha temple we saw yesterday.

Today on the boat Cornelia met an Italian plastic surgeon who propositioned her to spend time with him in Bangkok. He could speak ten languages and he sorts out the people whose plastic surgery has gone wrong. He disappeared as soon as we landed like a vampire from Bram Stoker's *Dracula*!

It was beautiful to float along the vast river, Irrawaddy today. It was beautiful. It was crossed by only three bridges and two of them were in Mandalay. The other was a vast bridge in thirty segments. It was interesting to watch the little life which existed along the riverbank. The river is beautiful but the country side as a whole is very neglected. There is human litter (packages, bottles, discarded rubbish) at all the sites, museums and stupas. It seems strange that in such a traditional society public space is not valued or cared for.

We got off the boat here in Bagan and had to climb up a very sandy bank with our luggage to meet a driver from the hotel. This was rough. We had to call into a tourist office and buy a ticket for the architectural heritage sites. This is a tourist tax paid to the military, it seems. We drove a long way out of town, far from the ferry to get to the hotel.

The hotel is splendid and is built along the banks of the river. We are in a small cabin, like a mobile home, laid out like an American motel in the pretty gardens of the hotel surrounding a large pool and there are other log cabins on the far side of the dining area. After we checked in I walked down through the gardens to look at the sunset over the water. This is an amazing and beautiful setting, so different from our city locations in Yangon and Mandalay. We ate here this evening.

Lazy Traveller Blog 12

March 12th 2012, Bagan Thiripyitsaya Sanctuary Resort

This lovely resort hotel must be owned or jointly run with a Japanese company, Sakura. The central hall is a pagoda which reminds me of the golden pagoda in Kyoto and in the far corner of the garden I found this morning while I was walking around before breakfast a Buddhist monument celebrating a tea ceremony which Japanese and Myanmar Buddhists had as an act of reconciliation and bridge building between the Japanese and the Myanmar and between the two forms of Buddhism. I had not registered until yesterday that Japanese Buddhism belongs to one major stream of Buddhism whereas Myanmar Buddhism belongs to the other stream. I am not sure of the differences but it feels as if the one we can see in Myanmar is closer to Hinduism and Tibetan Buddhism, with the monks dressed in plum red whereas the Japanese form, and perhaps the Chinese form of Buddhism also, is closer to Zen Buddhism. I remember the monks in Japan dressed in black and having very elegant circular offering bowls and straw hats. The story of Buddha seems to remain the same.

Today I am spending some time catching up with this blog. Cornelia headed off before dawn yesterday to find a stupa to sit on and watch the sunrise. She did the same this morning but it has become cloudy and so the sunrise was invisible. Perhaps this is a time of the year as the heat gets hotter and hotter before the rain and monsoons appear in another few months when it becomes cloudy. Something similar happened last night. We found a stupa to climb onto with many other tourists, young monks, and very pretty young female nuns. We all looked out towards the river. For a while it was very beautiful because the sun was a large orange blazing ball and this fire was reflected in the water of the river below. But then the sun crept behind a large cloud and disappeared. We still had a great view and it was a great thing to do. You have to catch sunsets when you can.

On the boat up from Mandalay we had a lovely sunset. Sunsets on water always look good although the speciality here in Bagan is to see the sun rise and set over a horizon and landscape filled with a variety of amazing stupas, temples and brick and golden constructions.

Yesterday because there is so much to see and we were a little lost we arranged to have a guide and a driver who could negotiate all the variety and lead us from one spectacle to the next. The guide was a young man in his mid twenties who was trained as a physicist. There is no call for physicists in downtown Bagan, sadly. His English was very elementary and his knowledge of the monuments and even the details of Myanmar history and the construction of the monuments was very elementary too. I think he had a frustrating time. He spoke a lot but his language was mainly incomprehensible. After a little while we were following the book and him, getting more from the book. But he did a good job getting us to places we would not have been able to find and by the end of the morning he was showing us amazing temples with incredible wall paintings.

We started off with a view from a stupa and then headed into the local market. Bagan is a quiet country place, despite the daily influx and departure of tourists. Presumably tourism is the mainstay of the local economy but this is a rural area. The market was filled with young women who had arrived early in the morning from the country with their vegetables to sell. They had arranged them in wonderful and creative ways and all the produce looked fresh and fascinating. No produce was to be taken home so prices were going to drop later in the afternoon. We saw green mangos and baby aubergines, women cutting these vegetables with huge cleavers into tiny strips for stir frying, stalls filled with an amazing array of fish and shell fish from the river and women gutting and preparing the fish for customers. Lots of local textiles were for sale and there were young women with sewing machines ready to make up anything anyone needed. It was a lively and rich place with monks wandering through at that time of the day with their offering bowls. Some of the monks are very young boys and their offering bowls were topped with candies.

In some of the other places the monks see so many tourists that they had little interest in interacting with us but yesterday was quite different. At one temple a monk wanted his picture taken with us. He had a camera! In another he was visiting the temple with his mother and sister and he asked us to stand with his mother and sister for a photo. They all merge into a mythical archetype of "monk" and they are only differentiated into old monk and young monk.

At the market, because it is the hive of local activity, we saw more people begging than elsewhere and these people were not necessarily focused on tourists. They were people with speech disabilities who had to beg and there were older people who clearly were quite distressed and were begging. We were told that the older people, if there are no families, can retreat into a monastery. Although Bagan is full of ancient temples and shrines we did not visit a monastery where monks live. As we saw in Yangon, which now seems a long time ago, at the start of our journey, the monasteries are simple places, often just made up of shacks and makeshift buildings. These are communities but they are not as elegant as the demeanour and style of the monks would suggest. These are poor places close to the breadline. The monks are part of the poor of the country, although at least the young monks are choosing their poverty.

The market was a rich surprise. It was interesting to see the rural life of the place and the energy and tone of all that was happening. The women both sold and bought most things. The men are in the fields or elsewhere making money. marketing, buying and selling to one another and to foreigners is a task left to the women.

We seemed to visit a lot of temples and I don't think I can remember them all even now. The names were hard to grasp but the variety was very good. In Yangon and Mandalay we have seen many temples and shrines but they were mainly very popular places which are still places of worship and ritual and have been updated in line with contemporary requirements for flashing lights, tv screens showing the face of the idol transmitted into the audience halls so that women can see the face of the Buddha, and the painting of the sculptures has been simple and garish as in Hindu temples. Bagan represents a more distant era and there are too many of these temples for them all to be places of worship. Most of them are just cultural ruins and have been left to decay for centuries. Some of the large places which have internal spaces have retained a life of worship and have adapted. We were told that Bagan became the religious and cultural capital of the country of Myanmar when a king who united the country decided that Buddhism would become the national religion. He sent to India for Buddhism and brought the scriptures and relics to this place around 1,000 AD.

We know from the story in Yangon that Buddhism had appeared in Yangon 2060 (or 2600?) years ago, shortly after the Buddha had been enlightened. The reality seems confusing and messy, like history generally. Buddhism may have made an appearance in Yangon but it needed some support from the state and a conquering king for it to become the religion of the nation and for it to accrue so much wealth and attention. This happened in Bagan around the 11th century. I think there were waves of development in this national, religious and cultural enterprise but we did not get that story yesterday. We were told that this was all 11th century and none of what we saw was differentiated and yet we saw very distinct things which had developed in amazing ways.

One place, Shwezigon Paya, was very like a smaller version of the big golden stupa we had visited in Yangon (where we had participated in the winter moon festival) and this one had more hairs of the Buddha and even a collarbone. It seems that Buddhism in Myanmar is like Medieval Christianity and both value relics and fragments of the holy one. The relics bring the supernatural power of the person and the past into the present and these relics ensure that sacred power is entertained in these places of pilgrimage. Pilgrims are attracted to power and origins and these relics are symbolic containers of pure numinous power, the holy and the sacred. This was a large multi-layered stupa which starts off as a square or an octagon (a square, in this case, I think) and then rises through various terraces until it turns into circles and various shapes and ends in a metal crown at the top. Around the edges of the stupa are featured additional niches with Buddha images or, as in this case, ideal and stylised representations of lotus blooms.

This temple was meant to have four large standing images of the Buddha which are venerated but we did not see these. Instead we found in some of the outer pavilions images which brought to mind different moments in the Buddha's life and journey. These were new and fascinating. In one the young prince Siddhartha was on his horse leaving the palace to discover the world. What he finds is old age, illness and death. These were represented by wooden figures on pediments, as you would see in a medieval cathedral. These were a surprise and quite fascinating. In another tableau made out of plaster and very crudely painted, Buddha was represented in prayer being tempted by demons. There was a huge sea monster appearing from plaster waves. There was a dragon being ridden by a demon. A woman as a demon (Mara?) made an appearance. The Buddha remains calm before these temptations and in front of him arises a single beautiful lotus, out of the mud. Out of the mud of our existence, full of suffering, decay and death can arise the miracle of beauty and enlightenment, the Buddha mind. In yet another pavilion, Buddha was preaching his dharma (teaching, I think) to five disciples. The guide was troubled by disciples and disciplines. I had not thought the two words could be linked, other than through derivation, but perhaps they are.

This temple was interesting but no different from others we had seen. However we moved on to others which were far more fascinating. In some there were four-faced images of the Brahma sculpted in stone on four pillars hidden within a dark space. We were seeing new currents of architecture and new experiments in the lintel and the arch. It was not clear where these new innovations and possibilities were coming from but it was fascinating to step into these ancient dark mysterious spaces and see both the new possibilities of interior dark womb like spaces opened up for the first time by the arch and other forms of technical innovation and feel the new space which was created by these innovations. We have been walking around the outside of stupas. We have been looking into small niches guarding single idols or blocks of stone on which has been written the scriptures. And we have been entering wooden structures on stilts, which are developments of the vernacular houses on stilts we can still see in the country. But these internal dark womb-like spaces represent something new and very exciting and it just got better and better.

At some stage this area was clearly a centre of innovation and experimentation in temple building, because there was a demand and money to keep on experimenting with temple after temple. We saw the interior spaces getting bigger and bigger until they were cavernous and cathedral like. We saw the walls getting thicker and thicker to support the larger and larger structures but we also saw openings appear to let in light and we gradually saw these fretworked stone apertures being used more and more accurately to define light and shady spaces within the interior. The architects learned to direct light onto the main idols. We saw them learning about acoustics and opening in the walls additional niches to deaden the sound of too many pilgrims visiting the shrine. These niches were then filled with additional Buddha images.

Most miraculously we saw the temples and shrines come to life with paintings and new forms of representational life. This was a surprise and very exciting. Initially we were seeing the same scenes from the life of the Buddha we have seen incorporated in the terraces of the stupas as small square-shaped relief sculptures. The images from the sculpted squares were translated into painted images. But then this developed and we saw the walls come to be filled with images not only of the Buddha and his disciples but also local life. We saw wonderful images of the Bodhisattva.

The Buddha as an image in transition and development in his various poses seems always to be about states of consciousness, with each pose trying to articulate the possible meanings and nuances of enlightened consciousness. But these images are static. We then see the Buddha further articulating states of consciousness and new elements by changes in his fingers and the poses. Yesterday we saw a number of wonderful golden images of Buddha standing upright teaching with a small seed in his right hand held between his index finger and thumb, representing either the travails of the world or the solution to these travails and his other hand holding his cloak away from his body. But the Bodhisattva provides images of the Buddha consciousness returned to the world and doing things in a new way. I am more inclined to the Bodhisattva than Buddha. The Bodhisattva has got to show how this enlightened form of consciousness (i.e. humanity at its best) can negotiate the world, make a contribution and survive in the midst of human travails. It is an active form of consciousness. We have not seen this represented elsewhere in the temples and stupas we have seen in Myanmar.

I wonder what all this means, if anything? Has Myanmar and religion retreated from action in the face of its military rulers and its turbulent 19th century believing that an altered state of consciousness will bring a way forward? The monks today seem to represent something which is both national and yet opposed to the military regime and yet the monks do not show a way forward in any realistic terms. In the face of technology and the contemporary world has Myanmar retreated to a form of spirituality of otherworldliness? Having once been invaded by the British as a colonizing power and having ongoing troubled relationships with China (initially the Maoist regime and now the post-cultural revolution expansionist new China) has Myanmar concluded that a retreat to being and national isolation is the only viable means to survive? While the Buddhist heritage is at the forefront of cultural identity the understanding of any national story is very weak. The country still has religious history but very little secular history or heritage which is valued and celebrated. Myanmar does not feel like China, a country leaping into the 21st century and making it its own, for better or worse. If the 21st century belongs to China it does not feel as if it belongs to Myanmar, as yet.

What was so surprising yesterday being to see the evidence still in stone and on walls that things were once otherwise than they are now. The past contained moments of amazing innovation and experimentation, celebrating and realizing what was possible. Many of the other things we have seen, which are still alive in terms of popularity and ritual, actually ignore all of these moments of changed consciousness and innovation and settle for something quiescent. The monkish culture celebrates inner discipline but also external tradition and religious authority. There is no secular life on show; there are no heroes or heroines. The contemporary does not really exist except as trade and tourism.

We saw fascinating examples at last of Hindu influences at this time and one monument had been painted over in 18th century with new murals reflecting life in Bagan in 18th century as the Portuguese arrived! This was a story we had not heard about and it is hard to see the remnants of any Portuguese influence.

Towards the end of the day we visited a huge Buddhist shrine which was vast and had amazing internal spaces beautifully lit by stone windows. There were tall wooden gold Buddha images facing each cardinal direction. Two of the images had survived the large earthquake which had destroyed much of Bagan. The internal spaces were articulated like a Gothic cathedral. The outer layer was for ordinary worshippers and pilgrims, the middle space was for royals and the social elite and the inner space was for monks and abbots etc. The story is that the demeanour of the image changes as you move from one place to another. We tried this and it worked. From afar the wonderful large Buddha image was smiling whereas in the inner space the demeanour was far more quizzical, not smiling so sweetly and much wiser and deeper in some strange and enigmatic way. This was spiritual art and religious architecture at its best.

By this stage the Burmese were building amazing buildings using arches and lintels. This is 11th century and as the buildings get larger the mass increases because that is the only way to build high without something like the flying buttress. The walls are full of mass and the only way to transform this mass is to add sculpture and decoration and then gold and colour. Something new was needed for the next stage of architectural innovation.

But the temples in Mandalay and even in Yangon seem to put aside all these innovations. At some stage, Myanmar re-enters a dark age, gives up on these amazing experiments in interiority and culture. Architects and builders retreat to simpler older forms and, somewhat paradoxically, the cultural focus moves from the fascinating interior into simpler, more devotional and less complex exteriors. The experiment is abandoned as an exercise in innovation and decadence. There is a fall from a belief in the human and we see a retreat into devotion and pure consciousness. I wish I knew more about the story and what happened.

Lazy Traveller Blog 13

March 13th 2012, Bagan Thiripyitsaya Sanctuary Resort

Today, after yesterday's frenzy of temples and Mynamar-style pavilions, we are having a quieter day. Cornelia headed off to climb a stupa and see a sunrise, which did not materialise because of cloudy weather and has now cycled off with a German Mädchen for a bit more energetic sightseeing. We met for breakfast and we will meet up again later when the cycling is over for sunset viewing.

I wandered off to walk around Old Bagan. It has been a fun morning. Because it is overcast, although it is still hot, the heat is slightly better than it has been for the past two days. It is almost bearable but by 1130 it is time to creep into the shade and have some time to digest what is happening.

I have become a lazy traveller again and did not bother with any guidebook or map. There is so much to see and to enjoy I did not need a plan for today. As I walked out of the hotel I stumbled upon a local hut in straw with the men sleeping outside to keep cool and a horse grazing under the trees. There are many ways to get around Bagan and one of them is by horse and cart. I think I may enjoy this later today. The man jumped up and offered me the horse and cart but I was happy to keep on walking to explore on foot for a while. In Inwa we had a horse and cart who took us from the little ferry to see the sights of the old city. He chatted away to the horse who clearly understood him whereas we did not have any language in common. He wanted Cornelia to sit up on the box beside him and I was in the dog cart behind. I had forgotten how suspension in carts and vehicles is a major innovation and changes the comfort of the traveller completely. It was great fun being buffeted around in the back of the cart as he took us on unmade roads. We were slipping back centuries. In Bagan the horse drivers are much more part of the tourist infrastructure and so they can speak some English, perhaps more English than some of the official guides. A number stopped me this morning and chatted for a while before they understood that I did not need a horse and cart at the moment. They did a good job.

I visited a few small temples and found them interesting but at one when I arrived, the young boy whose tourist's goods were out on display for sale inside the temple was still asleep his head alongside a radio playing music. This was a big dark chasm of a place with two or three chambers and looking up both in the central chambers and in the side aisles you could see the remnants of wall and ceiling paintings. Nothing was clear or visible but this was ok. Unesco have not got to this temple yet and it may be nothing special.

As I was about to leave the boy turned into a ministering angel because he said I could go up the stairs if I wanted to. I did not think there was an upstairs. In a similar very large example of these temples yesterday we could say the stairs up to the next level but there was no access. The temple guardian led me to a small hole in the wall and following me for a while lit my way with his torchlight.

This was an amazing surprise. At one stage the temples had developed dark interior chambers but they had also retained the three-tier terrace structure finished off with a pineapple or acorn-like seven or nine-tiered stupa. I had assumed I had seen this temple by visiting only its interior. But this one also contained an exterior journey. As I came through to the light I was on the first terrace of a stupa, all alone, in this case and I could walk around the whole stupa and ascend the next two levels. This was a very interesting structure, initially taking us into a dark womb-like cavernous space, leading us from daylight through the dark as in a cave or a labyrinth to the audience chamber where there was a large contemplative Buddhas lit from outside with pierce stone windows. These spaces were once dark but covered with murals and ceiling paintings in vivid colours. At the heart of this internal space, the heart of this whole complex, there is a large Buddha, a symbol of pure enlightened and enlightening consciousness, with one finger touching the earth and the other hand at rest in his lap receptive. But then we travel through the dark walls along very narrow stairs and reach a different form of external light. We are located in a new sacred space around which we have to walk in circles, looking on one hand at images of the life of the Buddha (no longer here in this case) and on the other hand, at the amazing surreal Dali-esque landscape of Bagan full of stupas and religious towers. We have been transported to a heavenly cultural kingdom as well as the earthly and political kingdom of Bagan. These circulating stupa structures are all that remains of stupas now in Yangon and Mandalay since the underlying temple structure has been lost and discarded. This huge stupa structure with three tiers and a pineapple top must be a heavy weight for the building to carry and so the walls just get thicker and thicker.

It was a wonderful moment to walk around this rooftop stupa all alone looking out at the river, the other temples and stupas of Bagan, at the new archaeological museum below and far into the distance.

These structures are so large that they provide shade. I found a shady spot and sat down to finish Lisa Appignanesi's recent book, *All About Love: Anatomy of an Unruly Emotion*.

The landscape of Bagan is reminiscent in some way of India and the particular landscape of Bagan, for some unknown reason, brings to mind the Indian novel of E. M. Forster and the visit to this small temple was a positive moment that reminded me for some reason of the visit to the Malabar caves in that novel. Forster's moment was one of awe and dread which conveyed in an intuitive and direct way the full reality of India as an overpowering, demanding and mysterious reality. My moment was of quiet calm and contentment. And yet they were linked, in some way, not yet clear.

I liked a lot of this book. She combines in it some philosophy, some psychology, some social science and statistics and a lot of careful readings and insights from literature to reflect on the nature of love not as an abstract event but as an "unruly emotion".

In Tenby I had read and enjoyed Comte-Sponville, the French philosopher, on eros, philia and agape. His book is stunningly clear and bright, unlike the older work by CS Lewis on the Four Loves. I had talked about this book with Frank in Finchley before I came away. Lisa continued the debate but in a new key.

I liked her understanding of friendship and Shakespeare (Hamlet and Horatio as an example of positive and faithful friendship vs Falstaff and Hal as an example of an abusive and failed friendship).

I like her reading of Flaubert's *Madame Bovary* and her expert insight into Tolstoy's *Anna Karenina*, as contrasting studies in adultery by men deeply involved in the topic of what she calls triangular love. This was great stuff. She makes me want to go back and re read these books again.

Love is taken as a means of transformation and fairy tales, in one mode, show what such a transformation looks like, as does Ovid. And, of course, we can read these tales as metaphors and get a sense of the transformation required and glimpse in Ovid what happens when such transformations are incomplete or fracture. But that still leaves the simple question of what is the nature of the transformation which occurs when we love. It would be good to have a clear understanding of this, just as it is helpful with Comte Sponville to have a better understanding of different kinds of love. Comte Sponville has no sense of transformation or change.

Lisa quotes Simone de Beauvoir explaining one element of this transformation brought about by ecstasy and suffering, the suffering element of passion implicit in the passion of love:

"pain is normally part of the erotic frenzy: bodies that delight to be bodies for the joy they give each other, seek to find each other, to unite, to confront each other in every possible manner. There is in erotic love a tearing away from the self, transport, ecstasy; suffering also tears through the limits of the ego, it is transcendence, a paroxysm ... the exquisite and the painful intermesh." (34)

But Lisa also comes to an understanding of what Jane Austen means by the quieter transformation of love:

"If the search for the 'right' partner is a modern gloss on the theme (of *Pride and Prejudice* (1813)), Austen emphasized that success in the endeavour entails **inward adjustments** and **a recognition of one's own failings**: it is not only matter of behavioural ploys."

There is the understanding of the nature of the transformation which love brings about.

Jane Austen.

"Both her male and female characters undertake what we would now call the 'emotional work' of relationship, something the film versions inevitably make less clear. Both sexes, too, are in search of partners. Austen gives us various possible kinds of marriage, together with an ironical gloss on what 'rightness' may mean. Her principal heroine, Elizabeth Bennet, ... is initially greatly taken by the charming Mr Wickham. But her 'first impressions' prove faulty here, as they do in her assessment of her eventual Mr Right, Fitzwilliam Darcy, considered for a good half of the book to be a disappointing prig, overblown with pride in his superior status. ... Despite the real possibility of future insecurity, she refuses her first offer of marriage from the sententious and fawning Mr Collins. When Darcy initially proposes to her, stating that he does so against his will, she adamantly refuses him: passion is not enough to justify union with a man who manifests so much simultaneous contempt for those she values. Only when he has recognised his own lacks as Lizzy has hers, only when she garners an insight into his character as composed of more than pride, does she begin to fall in love with him. Judgement, good sense and some of those traditional virtues—generosity, just action, helpfulness, devotion—rather than an excess of 'sensibility' are always core values for Austen."

And Lisa concludes:

"The choice between one partner and another is not a matter of romance, but of argument and discussion, of shared values and hopes of the world"

Jane Austen seems to provide, via Lisa, more insight and clarity than the Buddha certainly about eros, which Buddha seems to dismiss as a naïve form of suffering. De Beauvoir and Austen don't see the suffering as inconsequential or naïve but as necessary components of change and transformation. Rilke and Rumi would agree with them. This is not an argument between Buddhism and the West and perhaps they are complimentary. It is enjoyable that a visit to Myanmar, in the way we have done it, necessarily involves contact with and so appraisal of the Buddhism that we meet here but alongside this external journey I have been accompanied by Lisa quietly reminding me of the treasures and insights of the western tradition.

In China, the figure of Kanon, the androgynous figure of compassion, is at the bright heart of most Buddhist temples in the central halls, after the fat and laughing Buddha and beyond the hall dedicated to the teaching and ethical Buddha and the monkish spiritual figure of enlightenment. Kanon, not the Buddha per se, fills the heart with compassion and fellow feeling for other sentient beings. This presence of compassion has not been very evident in the forms of the Buddha we have seen in Myanmar. The Kanon legend in China combines a local fairy tale story (entailing a figure like Psyche suffering from love) with Buddhist concepts and iconography. She does not come to Myanmar, or we have not met this figure yet.

Perhaps in the Myanmar Buddhist tradition the figure of compassion is symbolised and comes to consciousness through the Bodhisattva, but even this figure has not been very noticeable.

Lisa's take on E. M. Forster in this context provides a Western update on Kanon and the Bodhisattva:

"In *Howards End* (1910), E. M. Forster gave his heroine the phrase which summed up the new ethos: '*Only connect*'. The understanding of the good life had shifted. The personal, the relational, the passionate—which also permitted congress across class and even gender lines—now weighed more heavily in the human balance than tradition and social convention."

The words are so simple and beautifully metaphorical but they calm and provide inspiration and direction.

We come on journeys with questions, which are often unclear and rarely articulated. They drive us in some strange way to seek answers for questions we cannot properly formulate. In some way it is Lisa's book which provides the answers to the questions posed by Myanmar but I am still not sure I have understood the question.

Lazy Traveller Blog 14

March 14th 2012, Inle Lake, Princess Resort

This morning I have got up early to write some notes about yesterday before Cornelia wakes up and we start a day looking around the lake. Yesterday we moved from the flat sandy spaces of Bagan which is on the Irrawaddy to this large and beautiful inland lake on the central eastern side of the country. We have moved from a dry desert-like land filled with thousands of old stupas and shrines from 11th century with some brush vegetation in bright green and dried yellow to the swampy area at the edge of the lake below a vast and gracious range of mountains. At this time of the morning, just before dawn, the vegetation around the lake is filled with the sound of birds and other animals beginning to sing and come to life. the geckos hidden away in the roof suddenly burst into their clicking sounds to remind us that they are quietly on the hunt for mosquitos. This feels like mosquito territory with large areas of swamp on the edge of the lake.

The hotel is built on the edge of the lake around a number of pools which have been filled with decorous water lilies. When we arrived the water lilies were in full bloom but in the evening I noticed at sunset that the blooms of the water lilies close and return to buds. Around the hotel wander two cats, one ginger and the other a beautiful Burmese blue-grey cat. Today we may visit the monastery with the jumping cats.

At the far end of the compound is the spa which is reached over a long teak bridge across the water lily ponds. Each spa treatment unit is a suite of rooms and there are perhaps four of them. Cornelia is going to indulge this afternoon when we get back from cat-watching.

There is a back entrance for staff to the hotel and I wandered to what they call the village yesterday evening just before sunset to see what this village was like. Part of it is a huge kitchen garden which is used to grow the fruit and vegetables used in the dining room and the rest of the "village" is the accommodation area for the staff. This is poor and very basic, in complete and stark contrast with the facilities within the hotel. The staff were out playing volley ball and enjoying their time off, getting ready to get dressed in their evening outfits for service in the dining room. This inequality should bring about some unpleasantness and resentment but the young people are very pleasant and there seems to be no rage against this inequality. Clearly there are very few opportunities of any sort in this area. We came from the airport to a small town where we transferred from a rickety taxi to a small boat. The town was also very poor. We have passed through a lot of poor areas in Burma and very little of anything above the very lowest levels of subsistence. This is a country still struggling to get its people out of the lowest level of dire need.

In the afternoon we sailed in the boat with our driver along the lake to see how people lived and get a sense of the human ecology of this lake, swamp area. It was meant to be a picturesque experience as we wandered around houses built from straw on stilts above the water and as we passed by single fisher men working on their tiny boats working their nets with both hands and paddling the boat with their right foot tightly working a paddle. But it did not feel like healthy sightseeing. Our trips around these areas felt patronising and prurient as we watched people go about their daily lives, washing their clothes, playing with their children. We were intruders, perhaps welcomed for the foreign dollars we might use to purchase cheroots and lotus blossom silk. We were involved in the tourist gaze and it did not feel too good. In Bagan we were looking at the monuments as cultural artefacts. Here we were looking at the people, their way of life and their poverty and this was expected to arouse our delight and interest. It felt strange and odd. There was no anger or resentment but it felt odd for us to be encased in a paradise like compound only wandering out to see the local people being picturesque.

The lake is beautiful as most lakes are. The mountains around the lake are magnificent. The birdsong and natural wild life which fills the lake seem amazing. It might be much better if we were here as tourists keen to see, appreciate and enjoy the birds or the vegetation or the cuisine. This is a subsistence culture and it does not feel appropriate to be watching people barely survive.

At dinner last night in the hotel we met the English couple we met at the start of our journey in Yangon. They had done a different circuit but we had visited many of the same places. They were full of joy and delight in their experiences. And when I asked them for their highlight of the journey they said it was the last few days they had spent in Inle Lake. They had enjoyed visiting local villages and meeting people at the markets. It was good to share their joy and delight. They had ended up without cabins on a two-night cruise along the Irawaddy, because the travel company had overbooked the boat and their rooms had been allocated to a larger French tour group. The agents had put them up with the crew. It was a terrible story but none of this phased them. They were delighted and had wonderful and mad stories to tell. I enjoyed talking to them a lot (much more than watching young girls making cheroots which are going to end up killing them).

There is a small library here in the hotel and Cornelia picked up an old volume called *Burma Tales* (or *Tales from Burma*) from the library. These are first-hand accounts of Burma in 1840-1880s told by old Burma hands. It was fascinating to dip into these stories and to read about how difficult this place was for so many Europeans and to realise how little has changed. The stories showed how resilient and resourceful these early colonisers had been. One woman came to be with her husband the captain of an oil boat sailing up and down the Irawaddy. As the only woman on board she had never left the ship and could only talk to a few other people. The heat must have been very bad but her story includes her admiration for her husband's skill in learning to navigate the difficulties of the river. There is no resentment and no sense of injustice or grievance. These are amazing and compelling stories of human strength.

I was saying that I needed more background to Burma to make sense of what I had been seeing. The pieces did not connect. I had no sense of the underling narrative, what had happened and why. Our guides were not able to articulate any of this for us. Our British friends recommended A *Travellers Guide to Burma* by Gerard Abbott. The Burma tales told of oil and teak and we found yesterday that Burma is the second largest supplier of opium in the world. I wonder if Burmese opium moved along these rivers to reach China and was it Burmese opium, planted and cultivated (by whom?) which resulted in the first and second opium wars in China.

After an afternoon on the water and an amazing sunset looking out at the sun setting over a wonderful range of mountains and listening to a great variety of birds we had our best dinner of the trip. This hotel has a good chef and a fantastic menu which was very interesting. The meal was delicious although still simple. The poverty of the country seems reflected in some way in a thin cuisine, in comparison with the amazing variety and richness in Thailand, India or China despite the fact that we have seen plenty of fresh produce in the markets. Something strange happens and there is very little flavour and interest in spices and flavours. For example I had a pea soup last night. I was intrigued what this might be like. But the basis for all soups we have tired here is a simple, somewhat unappetising but very wholesome lentil soup. Sure enough, this pea soup was lentil soup keen to be recognised as pea soup. It was good despite its appearance; the bread was home-made (although this is not a bread country), warm and delicious and the desserts with pineapples and bananas on a puffed-pastry base with ice creams were the best we have had.

Perhaps the strange moodiness and tawdry feeling belonging to the arrival in Inle Lake yesterday is a reminder of a few things.

I am missing my family and friends. It is strange to be so out of touch and it hurts at this stage, ten days in the strange world of Myanmar. Being out of touch helps me to realise how big a role they play in my life and how strange it is not to be in daily communication. This does not feel good.

I am reminded how much I enjoy lakes and mountains and water. Inle Lake reminds me of Venice, of places in England and Scotland, of Lugano and Locarno in Switzerland and the towns around Como in Northern Italy. I love lakes and mountains. I don't need the added zest of the exotic which Myanmar and Inle Lake provides to this concoction. A lot of pleasure comes from being close to mountains and water. I should do more of these visits but not necessarily in Asia but in the UK and in Europe.

The exotic is fascinating but it needs to be in some way more advanced than the UK and Europe. Poverty and stepping backwards does not feel very comfortable and cheapness is not a reason to visit poorer places. Physical poverty is not comfortable to gaze on as a wealthy foreigner. It feels wrong.

Tourism is contaminating. Luxury hotels in poor countries may be a necessary evil but that does not make them any the less contaminating.

I am reminded how much I enjoy the pleasures and richness of London. While we have been here in Myanmar we have had almost no music. We have had a lot of Buddhas but it is hard to beat great art to raise the spirits. London has so much and it is relatively easy to access. I am living in the right place. Visiting Myanmar might be fun but it remains a hardship assignment although I can imagine that if one gets to know local people the experience would be completely different. We have had a very false and hermetically sealed experience. We may have seen the sights but we are a long way from the heart of Myanmar.

The Buddhism here is so different from Buddhism in China, Japan and Bangkok. Beyond its elegance and calm I am not sure that as one of the major institutions in the country it does not take a fair amount of blame for the current state of poverty of its people. The monks and Buddhism had huge potential power. It is not clear they have used it wisely. I have not seen evidence that they have pushed for more literacy, 3rd level education, improved basic health care, rights for minorities and women, transparency and ethical values in public life, self-expression through art and culture,

The environment is being destroyed very quickly. It is not clear that this speedy deterioration can be blamed on foreign influence. At a basic level there is no reason for the roads and temples to be so scattered with discarded litter. This lack of concern for the basic environment

Lazy Traveller Blog 15

March 15th 2012, Inle Lake, Princess Resort

Last night we found two sets of ear plugs in our room with a note from the hotel which said that we were now in Buddhist Lent and we might be disturbed by the sounds of monks chanting during the night but since this was an important local custom the hotel could not do anything about it and the earplugs were provided to help us. I was waiting to hear the sound of the monks chanting and we may have heard something faint around 10pm but there was little sound. This morning as we were heading for breakfast around 0700 a bell was sounding from across the lake. It sounded as if this was a call to prayer or some part of a service. It was a beautiful sound. In the temples and shrines there are always many bells and gongs but these are for people who want to strike the bell as a form of prayer (as in Tibetan Buddhism); ringing the bell is another way of offering worship. The sound of the bell this morning sounded more regular and went on for a longer time. The bells in Myanmar are tuned to very musical notes in comparison with some European bells which sound blunt and unmusical.

We are leaving here in a few hours but I have some time before breakfast to write a few notes on all that we did yesterday. This was our full day on the lake and it went well. we had a great time and enjoyed many of the same things as the day before but whereas that trip on the lake seemed dull and listless yesterday's trip was very good.

What were the surprises and delights?

The trip across the lake was a surprise. It could not have been more different than the day before although everything was the same. We left early morning when the weather is still a bit cold. We knew we needed to keep warm for a while as we crossed the lake and we would have to be covered at midday because the sun was so strong. We wrapped up well and a new driver arrived in addition to the man who arranges the boats. He appeared on a bicycle to check with us that everything was alright with our arrangements for yesterday and our departure arrangements today.

The fishermen were out on the lake. This is the image Lonely Planet use for the front of their guidebook. Each fisherman is on his own small boat. He has to steer and move the boat with his leg wrapped around the paddle in a strange way. He is standing on the prow of the boat. He has to drop the nets into the water and leave a stake to remind himself where the net is. The water is very shallow, no more than a few feet. The fisherman then moves away from the net and starts to beat the water with his paddle to drive the fish away from where they are and into the open nets. It was fascinating to watch them and to see them all lined up ready to fish.

On the other side of the lake the fishermen were dredging the water and collecting green stuff from below the water. I don't think this is seaweed because the lake has fresh water but it is lake weed that you can see just below the surface all over the lake. The fishermen were dragging vast clump of weed from the water and loading them onto the same small boats. We were told that these weeds will be used for fertiliser on the floating gardens, which are drills of plants planted in some soil on the surface of the water itself. Next to the plants there are stakes and the plants locate themselves in the soil and creep up the stakes nourished by the weedy fertiliser. In the morning we saw the fishermen collect this form of fertiliser and in the afternoon we crept along the floating gardens and saw the men and women working on the drills, creating new drills, planting new specimens and caring for others. We saw tomato crops which were now in fruit.

This was all very agricultural and very interesting. On the far side of the lake the water was full of many boats all being piled high with this pond weed. Later in the evening, after sunset when we were walking to dinner we saw bright lights on the mountain behind the hotel. We asked what this was and we were told that the remnants of the sugar cane were being burnt in readiness for new planting. It made an amazing sight to see this bright orange fire lit up whole stretches of the mountain side. It reminded me of the custom celebrating Lughnasa which is discussed in *Dancing at Lughnasa* by Brian Friel.

When we got to the far side of the lake we entered a much smaller inlet which was the way to a market at the village of Inthein which was our destination for the morning; the water in this inlet seemed to rise from the level of the lake to the far higher level of the village at the foot of the mountain through a series of small dams or weirs which had been built in the river. These were made from bamboo and seemed to hold the water above at a higher level and yet in the middle of each of these weirs was a small gap and the boats sped through these gaps like salmon jumping up river. It was very exciting to approach these weirs at quite a speed and then zip through them, almost miraculously. The water remained in the weir at the higher levels and yet the water seemed to flow. I suppose the water was flowing down from the mountain into the lake.

It was also curious to see life along the river bank. Water buffalo were buried into the water up to their noses bathing. Children were bathing. Others were walking along the bank one by one with round shaped hats and panniers across their shoulders. The soil in this place was not like the soil on the lake which is black but here it was rich red and sandy. This whole experience of seeing these lake side villages, floating garden and houses on stilts was like seeing Venice being formed two thousand years ago. Here you could see the process of a place, a human place and a city or a town appearing out of the water, dwelling space being formed out of nothing and floating on the lake surface. It looked quite miraculous and it was possible to see how this process would lead to the Grand Canal with its many churches and fine palaces. In the middle of the lake someone had already built a large Chinese-style house which was far grander than anything else on the lake but had now been abandoned.

Eventually we ended up at the foot of a mountain which has a temple and a garden of very old pagodas at its base as well as a local market. This is the market which floats (not literally) around five locations on different days of the week. This is the furthest down the lake it appears. This market was nowhere near as large as the one we visited in Bagan but it was very enjoyable. It was filled with tribal people whom we had not seen before. These were more Indian looking mountain people. the women covered their heads with cloth in a shape reminiscent of a half-formed turban. The cloth was hand woven in bright colours made of cotton perhaps and looked like bright orange, purple and red tea towels. This was a tourist spot so the market had lots of souvenirs but it also had local produce, far less than in Bagan but this was a poorer place alongside the lake. An old lady full of smiles was sitting on her haunches makes tiny pancakes in batches of six. A bullock cart arrived down from the mountains driven by a driver and pulled by two beautiful grey brown animals. An old lady was sitting smoking a cheroot either very happy or slightly stoned. Women were washing clothes in the stream below the bridge and a pack of roaming dogs came down to get involved but were being shooed away by a man. The dogs were keen to participate in the market. The people with produce who could not afford a stall laid out their wares on a long line on white cloths. The vegetables and spices and rice all looked amazing. As in Bagan the stall holders and buyers were mainly men.

There was a covered walkway up the long path up to the temple. We went on a purchasing quest. Cornelia was interested in buying a Burmese opium weight in the shape of a lucky fish. We had found one of these tiny weights in Bagan at a souvenir shop packed full of local things. On the way up to the temple above Inle Lake a man appeared with many of these weights. On the way down however, there was a stall run by a lady who had many of these on display. But she had more. She showed us that these little weights were part of a set of six which were part of a scales. The scales—with both weighing pans, a stick on which to stand the two weighing pans and six tiny weights—were included in a small carved box. This was a mobile scales and weights. Perhaps these tiny scales were used for opium or they may have been used for jewels and stones. We were not too clear. But a deal was done and everyone came away happy.

We came down from the temple and continued to visit a silver making factory and a small place which made handmade paper which included pink and white leaves of bougainvillea. I thought this sort of paper came from India but we saw it being made on the lake from the pulp of mulberry leaves as a base paper. This place also included a few women with rings about their necks. Looking at these women with extended necks was too much like staring at local people as objects of exotic curiosity. We gave up on this place and had lunch at an exotic place on the water called the Golden Moon which sold wine made in Myanmar. We had seen the vines growing on the way in from the airport.

The last surprise of the day was at a temple on the lake called the Jumping Cat monastery (Nga Hpe Kyaung). The attraction is that the monks have trained some cats to jump through rings. It was fascinating. It was an interesting monastery made of teak on the lake, the only monastery we visited in Inle Lake. At one end inside the large temple on stilts above the water, a large circle of mainly women and children had gathered when we arrived. One woman (not a monk) was goading a black cat with a ring again and again. The cat walked away but she pulled it back. The cat did not seem too interested and wanted to get away. Eventually the probing by the woman who taunted the cat with a large ring which she banged on its head, led to the cat jumping through the ring held by the woman around two feet in the air. It was great fun. The cat jumped through the hoop and then got a fishy treat. Cat was happy. Once the cat had got into the groove it was willing to do a number of jumps as long as a fishy treat followed each jump. No fish treat no jump. The cat was clearly in control and the audience had no interest in the monks or the idols in this temple, just the cat. As soon as the cat had enough fishy treats the show stopped and everyone dispersed within seconds. The monk was left on his own, sitting on a throne, all alone.

I think I expected a large complacent furry Burmese cat to be on show and willingly doing tricks led by a big smiling monk dressed in plum red to delight the visitors. This was not the case. There was only one monk and he was placed beyond a large silver offering bowl. The cat trainer was a lady. These cats were not trained. They were as arrogant and as nonchalant as all cats but the jumping cat was willing to jump for its fishy treats. It was accompanied by a tiny kitten which apparently only had one eye and another rather mangy tortoiseshell cat. I think the offerings which the monastery received were as much to save the cats and give them some food as for the monks.

The jumping cat was not a big surprise, sadly. Amusing but not an amazing surprise, after all. But the monastery had a wonderful collection of temple Buddhas on altars. They were all displayed in a row as in a department store. It was a bit strange as if these amazing treasures had either been rescued or rifled from other monasteries or given as donations when monasteries were closed. Most of the Buddhist places we have visited had no such altars and idols. We have mainly seen large stone or bronze Buddhas but these altars were made in wood and were finely sculpted and decorated in gold and jewels. We did not have anyone to explain them to us but they were a very good surprise. We have seen temple carvings used to decorate the outside of monasteries and the roof finials but we have rarely seen wooden gilded carvings in temples. These were devotional images. It felt strange to see so many of them lined up together. Each was an idol in itself and required a full temple where it would be the centre piece and the major focus of worship for a community. It was as if these idols had been retired and this was a parking lot for retired idols (like film stars retiring to Florida and appearing in coffee shops). Or it was like the circuit over London where planes have to wait until they get a landing slot at Heathrow: these idols were waiting for someone to come and collect them and bring them to a new place of worship. Clearly they did not talk to one another, each stood in splendid isolation, oblivious of the other Buddhas and yet there was a certain sense of competition. This was a beauty parade of Buddhas, each idol fully made up and on display in its gilded altar vying with the others for glory, sanctity and power.

Some of the altars not only included the idol but golden monks prostrate in adoration or attending the dying Buddha.

This place on the lake with desultory cats and retired golden idols was a surprise.

Lazy Traveller Blog 16

March 16th 2012, Yangon, Governor's Residence

We are back in Yangon, currently the capital of Myanmar and getting ready to leave tomorrow very early. We travelled back from Inle Lake early this morning by boat to the main town off the lake and then by car to the airport.

We had only been there a few days but it was a great few days after a bumpy start. It was surprising to make the return journey and feel that it was so different. We pushed off from the hotel resort and a boy joins the boat to guide us out of the small canal on which the hotel is situated. He is like a barge guiding the boat, which is like a gondola, into the jetty. He takes the front of the boat and paddles the boat with his foot wearing trousers normally. This section of the journey is very still and quiet. The engine is not yet switched on and we were leaving around 0700 so it was wonderfully still. The lake was still misty and we had to wrap up warm because it was deliciously cold. The little boats have umbrellas to protect passengers against the sun at the height of the day and against splashing water at other times of the day. When we arrived in Inle Lake something was strange and it took a while to realise that here the men wear baggy cotton orange and yellow trousers not the normal Myanmar longhi, sarong-like garments we have seen elsewhere. It is unusual to see men wearing trousers. I wonder how long this will be the case.

When the steersman brought us out onto the main lake he is dropped off onto a small boat house where he and the other jetty boys seem to live and the engine is switched on and we were off. It was a wonderful journey past small tiny boats with one or two people starting the day and crossing the lake. We were a long way from the fisherman. We passed more floating gardens on the way, filled up with growing tomatoes. Sadly the tomatoes are not full of flavour. They are small and very bland. Perhaps Myanmar does not have access yet to better tomato seeds and plants.

Women were crossing the lake in the small boats sitting on their haunches perched on the edges of the boats in coolie-style hats, which are very practical.

This part of the journey was a lovely surprise whereas the car journey to the airport was horrid. We had the same driver as we had on the way to Inle Lake. He had not changed but his behaviour was more noticeable this time. He was an inveterate honker and let every bicycle, pedestrian and car on the road know that we were close by honking the horn. The journey took an hour. That was a lot of honking. We passed by crowds of poor people building the roads and we climbed up the side of the mountains we had seen at the far edge of the horizon at Inle Lake. The driver was a betel nut chewer and had to stop for a fresh supply of betel nuts from a waiting betel nut boy. The smell in the car was very bad. This was the first smelly surprise of the day. It was not clear if the smell was caused by the petrol fumes from other cars, the petrol supply was leaking and the car was filled with the acrid smell of petrol or the betel nuts smelt like petrol. None of this was clear and the driver belonged to the Myanmar mafia and wore dark shades, a high-necked jacket and continued to chew. We were pleased to arrive at the airport and leave the betel nuts behind.

However the second smelly surprise of the day was the smell in the gents. Wow! This was strong. This was the smell of urine raised to the power of five. The Burmese have a way with smells.

The flight went well however and only took forty minutes or so. We landed back in Yangon but had a very different sense of the place now that we had seen other parts of Myanmar than we did when we arrived from Bangkok so many days before. We found a driver and he brought us to the Governor's Residence where we were staying for the night and agreed to collect us the following morning for our flight from Yangon to Bangkok.

The Governor's Residence was the most luxurious hotel we stayed in and the room was very nice. It had a pool which was filled with people when we arrived around lunch time. at this time of the year the heat is at its most intense from 1130 until 1500. it is important to creep into a corner during this period. By 1500 it has become balmy and pleasant outside the city.

We went to the National Museum which had been closed on our first trip. This was a surprise in many ways. It is an appalling museum of the most old-fashioned and soviet style. Most of the ground floor was filled with presentations and rubbings of Burmese script. This was impenetrable but this section included one photograph of a scholar and it struck me that apart from images of the Buddha and some monks we have seen very few depictions of anyone while we have been here. There are no images of heroes, great figures from Myanmar's past and the military leaders seem to keep a low profile. We saw no images of musicians, actors, footballers, stars, singers, saints or scholars. We were saturated with images of the Buddha and we were deeply impressed by the many wonderful Myanmar people we met all over but we took away no images of people belonging to the nation of Myanmar, other than the famous lady. It seems strange for a country to be devoid of human images.

There was a large display on the ground floor about the Royal Palace in Mandalay. This was also very strange. The Museum contained the lion throne from the Mandalay Palace which was used by the last king of Burma. The throne had been taken to Calcutta by the British to be displayed in a museum there but was returned when the country gained its independence from the British in 1948 and the transfer was arranged by Mountbatten. The other thrones with the rest of the palace had been bombed and destroyed during the Burma campaign. It was strange for this throne to be the only genuine element of the palace to have survived. There were depictions of the other eight thrones and an explanation of the ritual surrounding the use of each throne.

Cornelia has been reading *The Glass Palace* by Amitav Ghosh, whose father was an Indian Burmese. The Glass Palace is the Royal Palace in Mandalay and the book depicts the final days of the last Burmese king and the details surrounding the exile of the king to India by the British. She has also been reading George Orwell's *Burmese Days* which is all about the teak trade in Burma. Orwell had been a police sergeant in a hill country town based on the teak trade. These books, work of ostensible fiction but well researched and beautifully written give a better sense of the palace than the strange lifeless artefacts we saw at the museum.

Each national museum has an agenda which it is conveying by its selection of images and stories. This national museum of Burma was very strange. The regime must have decided to exclude Buddhism as a strong and major influence, perhaps because they represent another sense of national identity. The monks did not make an appearance in the museum other than for the craft artefacts associated with their lifestyle. They had been airbrushed out of national history. Somewhat surprisingly the focus was on royal history and we got a better sense of the different epochs of Burmese history from a few diagrams than we got elsewhere in the country. Burma was alive and doing things in 13th-17th century. Our guides had focused on 11th, 12th century and then we always jumped to the 18th and the arrival of the British. We did not get very coherent narrative anywhere in Myanmar and it was not much clearer in the museum, which was a moribund and sad place.

There was a room of marionettes and musical instruments. These musical instruments and the dances which the music accompanied must have played a very important role in the cultural life of the nation. We had heard and seen very little and the instruments were silent, the puppets were hanging like criminals from the gallows on which they were displayed. It would have been good to see all these instruments animated. It would have been good to have things to play. it would have been good to see this museum full of young people learning about their own culture but there was no one there most of the time we were there.

We were keen to get a feel of the tea house culture that is developing in Yangon we were told. We found a tea house and went in for something to eat and drink but it was curious. One table was occupied by money changers and people visited them from time to time. another table was filled with visiting Indian ladies and a local lady of ample portions who was entertaining them. No tea was being drunk. I enjoyed a plate of avocado salad with rich juicy grapefruit. It looks as if the strawberry season has just begun. Huge mandarins and pomelos were for sale on the street.

We got lost on the way back but we had directions in Burmese and we found a cab driver who was able to get us back for a final lounge at the pool, drinks and then dinner. The hotel was luxurious but the food was only so so. The hotel in Inle Lake, we decided, had served us the best and most genuine food of the trip and the Indian food in Mandalay got a special mention from both of us. The breakfast in the Strand hotel in Yangon was superb and was not bettered on the trip. There I had a wonderful local fish soup with noodles for breakfast; the croissants and bread were home made and the jams and orange juice were delicious.

Life in Myanmar finishes early. We have been in bed most nights by 9pm. Will we cope with a return to a world where people are still busy at 1130pm?

A day of interesting surprise

Lazy Traveller Blog 17

17th March 2012, departure from Myanmar, Yangon, Governor's
Residence
And return to Bangkok and Four Seasons

This was our last day travelling together. Our trip to Myanmar was
coming to an end. We were both flying to Bangkok. Cornelia was then
flying via Hong Kong to the US and I was staying in Bangkok for a few
days to recuperate after the drama of Myanmar before I headed on to
Cambodia to see Ankgor Wat.

Everything worked out very well. We checked out of the Governor's
Residence and got to the airport in plenty of time. There was a man who
was going to change our Myanmar remaining currency into dollars at a
bad(ish) rate. The bank had not yet opened. Two young people came up to
us and said they were the bank and if we waited a moment or two they
would open the exchange and sell us dollars at the right rate. The older

man was content and shrugged his shoulders, "fair cop, guv" and the young people were a delight.

We had met only pleasantness and kindness from everyone on our visit. The hotels and guides and shop keepers, the waiting staff and everyone we met had been extremely friendly and very welcoming, keen to make a good personal impression but also proud of their country.

The book advised that we would have to pay an exit foreigners' tax, to be allowed to leave. We enquired about this one and there was a booth which had formerly sold these stamps but we took what she said to mean that this was no longer required. I suppose just as we found the people very friendly we also could not understand the English most of them spoke to us. They opened their mouths, as I open my mouth when I think I am speaking Chinese: words come out but they are incomprehensible. It would not be so bad if the person talking to us did not think they were speaking English but even when we heard them a second or third time it was still incomprehensible. And that level of poor English extended to the official guides as well. We met a few (literally three or four) young men who spoke amazing English and were acting as private guides. They had a good knowledge of the country and they were able to both discuss things and conduct a conversation. No doubt this level of English will come quickly but it needs a lot of effort injected into both the private and commercial world and the state education sector if there is going to be a fast change.

Cornelia did a great job organising this trip. As we sat at the gate waiting to leave the republic of Myanmar we were reflecting on the trip, relishing many of the details, hotels, people and sights and I was congratulated Cornelia on the hotels she selected, the route she had worked on, the travel arrangements finalised with a travel agent in Bangkok (perhaps). It was a miracle that we should both end up in Bangkok for this trip and we should both have sufficient time away from our homes to enjoy this trip into the cyber desert of Myanmar. We had been out of contact, for the most part, for the whole of the trip but we hoped everyone would still be ok. It is strange in this day and age to be cut off from email and mobile connections for such a long period of time. In China you can access email and mobile phones all over the country. In Myanmar this is not possible even in Yangon. But no matter, it was part of the charm that we could not make contact with the outside world.

Our flight back to Thailand went well and then after getting through immigration and picking up our luggage, Cornelia headed off to the Cathay Pacific first class lounge for some luxury and delights and I headed into town to check back into the Four Seasons for three nights of emails, connections and doing some planning for Cambodia.

We agreed we travelled well together.

The best hotel was probably the Strand

The best dinner were the Indian dinners in Mandalay

The best gimlets—not sure about that one

The best breakfast—the Strand

The best lake—Inle Lake

The best pagoda—the one in Yangon

The best temples—definitely Bagan

The best sunset—they were all good

The best sunrise—not the one when we left Yangon and Cornelia was ill.

The best jumping cats—still searching. We can do better.

Surprises—many many.

Would we go again? Not sure. The country needs a lot of work and it will take years and when the work is done it will change completely. We agreed that this was a fortuitous time to do this sort of journey when the numbers visiting are still relatively small. It is hard to see this place becoming a Bangkok but it will become a much bigger destination and its success attracting so many people to its strange mystique will result in that mystique being lost. At the moment it is still a place of innocence, a garden of Eden that has been frozen in a time warp for fifty or sixty years. For most of the country the 20th century did not happen. Their lives changed probably for the worst as a result of the war with the Japanese. It was not clear that the British did too much damage but they did not leave a legacy which withstood the onslaught of the Japanese war or the rise of the military. Buddhism has clearly defined the culture and the national temperament and has resulted in the general happiness of people but also their quietism. I wonder what will happen when more of them realise what they are missing out on and who may be responsible for this.

Lazy Traveller Blog 18

18th March 2012, Four Seasons and day at Ayuthaya in Thailand

I am back in Bangkok after a tough day of sight-seeing visiting the old capital of Ayutthaya which is about 85 kilometres from Bangkok. If this was a Cornelia trip there would have been a driver, a guide, a strong itinerary and we would have left on time and returned before the sun became too hot. But since Cornelia left for Hong Kong and New York yesterday I was back to my own resources today and decided to revert to type and go with the flow for the most part. The guide indicated that it was possible to do this trip by train but when I discussed this with the hotel yesterday there was an audible intake of breath and a shaking of heads. "I don't think so, sir" etc. But I managed to get them to put their credulity to one side and I managed to do the trip anyway on my own but not without some aggravation.

I decided to try to do as much as I could as early as possible before the heat became too intense and so that meant a 0500 rise. I have become used on this trip to getting up early. I am in the groove now. The 0500 start is painful for a few minutes but then I am fine. I left the hotel and headed for the main train station Hua Lamphong. I had not visited this place before. I was not sure how to purchase tickets, find the train and get off the train at the right spot. This was all exciting in a low-key sort of way. The station is a big old-fashioned station in the centre of town and a taxi dropped me there in less than fifteen minutes from the hotel. I hate dealing with taxi drivers usually and have consigned the whole lot to a very low circle of my personal inferno but this one was good and the roads were clear at that time of the day. I found a ticket window and the chap was able to sell me a dirt-cheap train ticket to leave for the right train to Ayuthaya around 0630. He even directed me to platform 7 which I found. Things went well. I even had time to get a latte and a dunking donut for the journey. The ticket told me that it was a standing ticket and the journey would last around 1.5 hours. I hoped the standing part was not correct.

I was travelling third class and the whole world was there and there were people shuffling back and forth from carriage to carriage selling water, fruit, soft drinks, fried rice and dried banana chips. Some people seem to have been on the train overnight and may have slept there. They looked tired and the children did not wake up for the entire journey. It was all fun. There was a mother and a daughter seated across from me. Yes, I did get a seat. And the little girl was thrilled with the windows which pulled right down. She was able to put her head out of the window into the breeze for the whole journey. This may not be allowed in other countries but all seemed well. The carriage was as rough and probably as old as some of the taxis we had used in Myanmar, provenance 1970 or so. On the way back I realised I could see the track below through the wooden slats of the carriage floor.

But the journey there went well. This was a nice surprise and I managed to negotiate the travails of the rail system at that time of the day to arrive in Ayutthaya around 0830 ready for some stupa and relic viewing before the sun became too hot.

The old city is now a small and quiet place surrounded on all four sides by rivers or canals. It is a Unesco world heritage site which has been looked after very well and there is plenty to see. I managed to visit Wat Phra Si Sanphet which has the stupas which were dedicated to three royal kings of Thailand or Siam when it was the major force in this region. This royal complex abutted the ruins of the old royal palace; it was a similar arrangement as the one is Bangkok. The palace had its own place of royal tombs. Most of Ayutthaya is now in ruins which have been carefully laid out with fragments of Buddhas in various states of collapse and the stupas and other structures are also in a state of collapse. In certain monuments outside the city perimeter the forest has started to reclaim the monuments and the Buddhas have become embedded in the growing trees. It is very beautiful. I visited this site in 1989 before I went to Japan but I remember it rather differently. It was interesting to return to the place.

I think I looked at Ayutthaya in the light of what I had seen in the last ten days or so in Myanmar. This was bigger, more complex and richer. Buddhism, royalty, state and people were linked.

When I came out of the ruin and headed next door toward the monastery with the large Buddha, Wat Phra Mongkhon Bophit, I met two elephants on the street with harnesses and saddles carrying tourists around the old city. There is a large elephant corral in Ayuthaya. Nevertheless it was a lovely surprise to come across happy elephants walking along the street. They are majestic and beautiful animals. They were part of the culture of Myanmar and Thailand in previous ages and now they have disappeared other than as a tourist spectacle. Amitav Ghosh in *Glass Palace* has some good sections on the work of elephants and what happens when elephants develop anthrax and how it was that the British used the innate intelligence and power of the elephants in the teak trade in a new way. Thailand and Myanmar had only used elephants for fighting and for display. Ghosh also talks about Myanmar women breast feeding the white elephant in the palace of Mandalay before it dies to signal the fall of Burma to the British. It was great to be reading Ghosh on elephants while visiting Ayutthaya.

The monastery has a large bronze Buddha which has been covered in gold leaf. I know more about this process from my time in Myanmar. Around the outer walls of the monastery were other bronze Buddha images in a state of being turned to gold by the gold leaf of worshippers. It was interesting to see this natural alchemical process taking place, base metal was being turned to gold by the worship and almsgiving of ordinary people over many years. This was a surprise and very thought provoking. In a small monastery on Inle lake we had seen three small Buddha idols which had been so loaded with gold that they had changed shape and were just round blobs, one smaller blob on a larger one, like a cottage loaf. The statues in half gilded state were very beautiful. In the city shrine close by this temple there was a pole which was being gilded by worshippers too. At the moment it was 80% red lacquer and only 20% gold and people were still adding golf leaf to the post. Over time many things end up being gilded, transformed from one realm of base matter to another of spiritual significance and value by the donations and imagination of ordinary people. This feels like a good process.

In the same temple I saw the eight forms of Buddha dedicated to the seven days of week with Wednesday morning and evening taking the number up to eight in total. In Myanmar we had seen the same daily images venerated by the person born on that day with water but in this monastery this veneration used coins, as if water and money and perhaps gold and light were interchangeable forms all possessing some liquid hermetic transforming intermediate quality. I realise I learned a lot about Buddhist rituals in Myanmar.

In addition to palaces and monasteries Ayutthaya has stupas and I looked at three of these and I was surprised. In particular I was surprised to learn more about Wat Phra Mahathat. This stupa has collapsed and is now in ruins but in the museum are displayed the treasures which were found buried inside the stupa in the 12th century. Walking around the stupa is interesting but it was very hot by the time I got there and it was hard to distinguish one ruin from another whereas the treasures displayed in the museum were air-conditioned for some reason although they are all made of gold. Looking at them was bliss. The museum presented them in the form of relics on an altar. The centrepiece of the city was a relic of the Buddha which the curators told us was one third the size of a rice grain, i.e. almost invisible. What was even more fascinating was to understand that this stupa with this relic of the Buddha was ground zero, the living and powerful centre of the capital and so the kingdom. Mircea Eliade writes about sacred geometry and sacred city planning. This was one of the few times I have seen these ideas really come to life. The palace and the royal tombs were located behind to the west of this centre of the city. Bagan had no such overall plan as far as I know although so many of the monuments were religious. And Yangon has its stupa but this is a British city focused on trade and administration not a traditional Burmese city. Bangkok replicates these ideas to some extent but they are not as visible or as clear as in Ayutthaya. This was a wonderful surprise.

The other surprise in a similar vein was the Wat Ratburana. This was a royal stupa or prang, and I had assumed these were structures with no interiors and so not burial mounds but just commemorative structures. That is true but things were buried in their foundations and because this monument was subject to earthquakes the things have been excavated and are now on display in the museum. The relics buried in the foundation of the prang was an exact replica of the prang, almost like a hologram in gold and precious jewels as well as Buddha images and betel nut instruments. It is interesting that these betel nut implements which are still in use today are the same but the ones included in the stupa were made in gold. The craftsmanship of all these objects was very fine and better than anything we saw in the Myanmar National Museum. The museum and these ruins brought all this to life, surprisingly and it was a revelation.

I pootled around looking at a few more things. The Buddha statues from the Ayutthaya period were splendid, really beautiful, created at the same time as the Angel of Chartres but more eloquent and more finely articulated.

Then I was tired and the sun was rising. I made my way back to the station but that was when the nats (Thai and Myanmar forms of spirits, often nature based and a bit mischievous) started to play. The train to

Ayutthaya was delayed in the morning by thirty to forty minute for some reason. This delay increased from train to train for the rest of the day and with each train seemed to be worsened. So I waited for the train back to Bangkok for almost two hours. I could imagine Cornelia going spare.

But after I got over the shock of now knowing if I was ever going to get back to Bangkok today since the arrival time of the train kept moving backward by thirty minutes very often, I settled down to read the *Glass Palace* by Amitav Ghosh and the time moved along quite pleasurably—honest!

When the train arrived it was very full and on the way back it took over two hours. It did not really help that the ticket for the train only cost 15 baht (there are almost fifty baht to the pound). It was cheap but boy was it hot and uncomfortable. However, Ghosh was a great read and I continued this novel about Burma, the end of the Burmese royalty, the last king of Mynamar who is exiled to India. At one stage in exile the king reads about the King of Siam who is making a European tour and being feted by the great European powers in the UK, Vienna and Paris. The King reflects that the Burmese are the ones who take over and lead to the collapse of Ayutthaya. Ayutthaya at its height is ruled by a Burmese monarch and yet Ghosh is right that none of this splendour goes back to Burma, which is viewed as the richest country in South East Asia for natural resources by the British and now the Chinese. It produces and exports more rice than any other country, had immense and valuable teak forests, gemstones galore and has natural oil and petroleum. I am not sure in comparison Thailand has any of these and yet now Thailand seems by far the richer country, partly because it is not at war with itself. It combines effortlessly royalty, Buddhism, culture, business, tourism, tradition and modernity. It is a model to be learnt from whereas Myanmar seems to have ended up in a backwater of its own making.

A day of Thai, Burmese and train surprises.

I was so pleased to arrive back at the train station in Bangkok and then catch a tuk tuk which drove me, via a stop at an Indian tailor, back to my hotel where I flaked out and tried to recover from too much heat. Today was my daytrip out of Bangkok. Tomorrow I plan to stay in town and get ready for departure to Cambodia on Tuesday.

W. Somerset Maugham has a book called *The Gentleman in the Parlour*, which is the "record of a journey through Burma, the Shan States, Siam and Indo-China". I like this book a lot. He is very good on the broken, fragile beauty and disappointment of Mandalay. His visit to Bagan is fascinating. Each chapter is very short, as if each is a product of one day, something like a blog. He says that the whole book is by way of a personal experiment for him. He makes great use of his material. Chapter 4 includes the following extract, which made me smile as I was reading it:

"Though I have travelled much I am a bad traveller. The good traveller has the gift of surprises. He is perpetually interested by the differences he finds between what he knows at home and what he sees abroad. If he has a keen sense of the absurd he finds constant matter for laughter in the fact that the people among whom he is do not wear the same clothes as he does, and he can never get over his astonishment that men may eat with chopsticks instead of forks or write with a brush instead of with a pen. Since everything is strange to him he notices everything, and according to humour can be amusing or instructive. But I take things for granted so quickly that I cease to see anything unusual in my new surroundings. It seems to me so obvious for the Burman to wear a coloured paso that only by deliberate effort can I make the observation that he is not dressed as I am. It seems to me just as natural to ride in a rickshaw as in a car, and to sit on the floor as on a chair, so that I forget that I am doing something odd and out of the way. I travel because I like to move from place to place, I enjoy the sense of freedom it gives me, it pleases me to be rid of ties, responsibilities, duties, I like the unknown; I meet odd people who amuse me for a moment and sometimes suggest a theme for a composition; I am often tired of myself and I have a notion that by travel I can add to my personality and so change myself a little. I do bring back from a journey quite the same self that I took."

Maugham's descriptions of Burma, the city of Rangoon, his boat trip down the Irrawaddy and his visit to Pagan (Bagan) are beautifully written. The initial part of his journey is similar to our own. However he constantly meets odd Brits who are expats on his travels and for the most part he listens carefully to their stories and these are what he includes in his travels. He is building material as a novelist for the future. He writes very well and as in the section above, he is full of insight about himself and those whom he meets.

Like Maugham I can say although I have travelled a lot, I am a bad traveller. I have not yet learnt the art of travelling well.

My sense of surprise is not quite the same as Maugham's. I can be surprised by many things; some of these happen abroad and there are many which happen at home. They are unexpected and often delightful. They indicate a different world from the one I am used to, they represent a challenge to my own perception of the world. They are the 'other' in some small way. They move me and my perceptions and they change my understanding and appreciation of the world. They are new facts which challenge my world view. They demand that I change my understanding in some small or large way. The world is not as I thought it. It is other, different, exotic and fascinating. A surprise indicates that I am in movement. I am about to be changed if I can take on board the content of the surprise. I am interested in these surprises on such a journey because there is an assumption, as Maugham outlines, that we are changed by a journey. But it is not always clear how such a change can come about. Catching sight of and respecting the surprises is one way of working along with the process of change offered by a journey.

Lazy Traveller Blog 19

19th March 2012, Four Seasons and a day of Bangkok pootling

We met a British couple in Yangon who said they had pootled around Myanmar for a few days before we met them. Cornelia and I discussed the word. I like it. Today I decided to pootle with no earnestness at all. Tomorrow I will be on the move again, heading to Cambodia.

Yesterday nearly killed me. That train back from Ayutthaya was really tough. There were four tracks in front of the station at Ayutthaya. The train back to Bangkok was leaving from third track. When I heard this I asked how to get across to platform three. The ticket seller looked at me and smiled. There were no platforms. There were four sets of tracks with a few feet to separate each of them. For a few hours while we were all waiting there was no traffic on the line. Then trains seemed to arrive; there was a flurry of activity. All up traffic arrived on the track nearest to the station. But then our train was finally signalled and we started to move across the tracks to line up for the train. It seems you can get on the train from both sides. Another train was hurtling through on track two just before ours was due to arrive. This caused a flurry since some foreigners were hanging around in the middle of track two. The guards moved us all along to the safety and chaos of track three until our train arrived.

The train was really packed on the way back and very hot indeed. Without a book it would have been hell. As it was it was hell but the book distracted me completely.

I decided that today I was not going to have a tough agenda and would pootle around Bangkok and see what happened. I have arranged the flights to Cambodia online with Air Asia. I was able to check in online this morning for the flight there and back and I was able to print out the boarding cards for tomorrow to make things easier. I did this after breakfast and I already felt I had had a productive day. I set myself a low target for achievement.

I have noticed there are now many more elephants appearing in temples. These are offerings. Perhaps this is the year or month or season of the elephant but the shrine dedicated to the four faced Brahma near to the hotel now has a whole herd of elephants waiting for blessing, offerings to the shrine. Some are large elephants (perhaps half life size) in gold and many others are in wood. They are being lined up pointed toward the main idol. I tried to ask someone today about these elephants at a street crossing but the person I asked had no clue what I was asking about. I will try again.

I crossed a canal along the street from the hotel before we went to Myanmar. I was intrigued. I found this small canal on the map and it looked as if this canal had various stops. I decided to experiment and take the boat towards the Chao Phrao. I was not sure where I wanted to go but I thought a canal trip would be an enjoyable start to the day. I got on the boat at Pratunam. I had worked out which way the boats were going, one side of the river was up the other down. The boat had perhaps twelve benches across the whole boat and you had to jump straight from the bank down onto the bench. It was like an old-fashioned railway carriage. The canal boat man stood on the six-inch edge and loosened the ropes from the edge and then jumped in leaning down to ask for the fares. A man next to me helped me out and told me that the fare was 12 baht (perhaps 25 pence).

The boat ride was good. We called in to a number of stops but there were no names on the stops. But it was not difficult to follow the map and I decided to jump off near something on the map called the Golden Mountain. The stop may have been called Phan Fa Lilat (or something). It looked an interesting area.

I got off and the heat was beginning to get intense. A tuk tuk driver tried to send me off to look at some giant Buddha but I was not too interested. I did a giant Buddha yesterday. Instead I wandered into an amazing place called Loha Prasat. This was an amazing place which was built in the 19th century but based on a model from Sri Lanka. This place was built on a square plan made up of many small squares of the same size, with a black metal roof. It had perhaps six stories. This was a house of wisdom which was meant for pilgrim monks where they could go away on retreat when the monsoons were very heavy. They were allowed to stay in this place. They stayed on the level appropriate to their level of enlightenment and disciplines. The top storey was a small relic house which contained a shrine with some relic of the Buddha. This floor was only one small square in size whereas the other floors were perhaps nine or twelve times the size of this individual unit. There was a spiral staircase going up the centre of this structure to move people from one floor and level of enlightenment to another. The ground floor (1) was perhaps where people slept, the next level was a library (2), the next contained images of the Buddha in various stages of enlightenment (3) (this level contained shrines and an external verandah), the next level (4) was for sitting meditation, the next for walking meditation (5), the next one described the levels of discipline required of saints (6) and then the top storey (7) was for the Buddha and his relics who presided over every element of this house of enlightenment. I have never seen such an amazing structure before. Most of the structures we have seen in Myanmar and here in Thailand have been for worshippers whereas this structure was for practitioners, monks and specialists. It was fascinating and had been curated very well. it was now an official Buddhist monument and had been finished off with lots of words of the Buddha written on the walls, great sculptures. Even in the intense heat this was a place of calm, shade and rest, perfect for meditation and spiritual work. Wind chimes had been attached to the roof eaves and so the whole building was singing beautifully. This structure of enlightenment was located next to a royal shrine dedicated by a king to his adopted daughter who had died in childbirth. The temple and this structure of enlightenment demonstrated the close links between Thai Buddhism and Sri Lankan religious ritual. We had heard nothing of these links in Myanmar.

As I was leaving this temple complex I bumped into some tourists and told them how wonderful Loha Prasat was and they should not miss it. I found it amazing but it contained almost nothing. It was an empty space for the most part. Its beauty was to do with simplicity and geometry. It did not have the gilding, mirrors and jewels of other Thai monuments. This lovely exercise in pure architecture reminded me of the great Sinan Mosques in Istanbul full of amazing geometrical features. I hope the others were not disappointed. The Loha Prasat could have come straight from an Escher drawing of infinity or Umberto Eco's *Name of the Rose*.

I visited Wat Suthat also, another huge temple complex which was close by Loha Prasat. This one was strange and surprising because it was filled with Chinese stone sculptures and there were nine Chinese-style pagodas each with nine levels on each side of the audience chamber. We had been told in Myanmar that Burmese Buddhism followed the Indian strand of Buddhism which was distinct from the Buddhism in Japan and China and certainly the monks and temples we visited in Myanmar were completely unlike anything I had seen in Japan and China and yet here we were in Thailand and this temple was filled with Chinese figures. Some of the temple guardians seemed to be stone sculptures of Europeans with swords and top hats. The guide did not explain what was going on but this was unusual and strange. Inside this temple in front of the main idol there were life size seated sculptures of perhaps forty monks, all painted and listening to the Buddha who was not a simple monk and who was represented perhaps three times life size. When I came into the audience chamber I thought there was a group of people praying and chanting so I crept around quietly looking at the murals. Then after a while I went closer and realised that these figures were all stone. This was very strange indeed. The figures were all individualised but they made up a large group and took up over half of the audience chamber.

By way of stark contrast this evening I picked up a new pair of glasses and headed to Asok to visit Asia Books. I am suffering withdrawal symptoms because I did not bring enough reading material with me. The guidebook recommended this bookshop which has been in Bangkok for a long time. This shop is on the Sukhumvit Road. I stayed along this road at the Ambassador when I first visited Thailand. The hotel was horrid and I have no memory of the place at all.

The bookshop was very good indeed. We should have visited before our trip to Burma. They had a collection of interesting and informative books about Burma. I could not bring myself to start a new book on Burma as I head into Cambodia. And the books on Cambodia all seemed to focus on the war. I have very little sense of Cambodia as yet but I am not keen to start reading about the killing fields as my introduction to a new country. I may call in again when I return from Cambodia. The bookshop was a great surprise and I picked up a volume by Nicholas Delbanco on *Lastingness: The Art of Old Age*. It is about older artists and the work they produce as they get older. This is a topic I am interested in and I am hoping that the book develops on from Edward Said and his *On Late Style*. However, when I started to read the introduction I found the writing style not very good—let me be polite. I am bringing it with me nevertheless to Cambodia. I have a long boat trip to Siem Reap from Phnom Penh. I may need reading matter when I finish *The Glass Palace*.

The first big surprise came when I got off at Asok and found a huge department store in the shape of a shipping or cruise ship terminal. The security guard in dressed like a sailor greeting you as a guest on board the ship. The different floors of the department store are linked to the ports the ship will visit. France is on the ground floor and I think Italy is on the lower floor. I was amazed by the whole thing. I wandered around France briefly but I was keen to get to the bookshop before it closed. I will have to go back.

In stark contrast with the lavish luxury of this mega department store was the walk to Asia Books along Sukhumvit Road. This was a gross surprise. Buddha would have been very distressed. Everything and anything was for sale and it was unpleasant. I don't remember things being quite as bad when I was here in 1989. It was a shock. I realise the area where the Four Seasons is located must be the Knightsbridge of Bangkok and this street market in Asok is Oxford St or the old Soho. Walking along this road tonight contrasted with this morning's pootling around Loha Prasat.

But I finished the evening with chicken in coconut milk soup and rice. It was great.

Time to get ready for Cambodia. This period in Bangkok has been restful and I am now feeling much recharged and ready to get to know a new South East Asian country.

Lazy Traveller Blog 20

20th March 2012, Four Seasons, Bangkok to Riverside Hotel in Phnom Penh

I had an easy morning in Bangkok before checking out at 1200 and heading for the airport and the short flight to Phnom Penh. Up to now things are going well. I managed to contact the hotel last night and asked for directions. They have agreed to send a driver for $10—that sounds good. Cornelia would be pleased with all of this advance preparation and general easing of confusion. I sent them a note and asked them about the boat trip to Siem Reap. It is not as long as the boat journey from Mandalay to Bagan and there are seats on board. It would be nice if the hotel could help me book it there and back. The boat leaves on Thursday morning so I have plenty of time to arrange this tomorrow if the hotel can't help. The hotel seems to be close to the royal palace and the national museum. I am hoping that visits to these places tomorrow plus a stroll around this evening will begin to give me a sense of Cambodia and how it differs from Thailand and Burma.

This morning I spent some time looking at the amazing luxury around me in Thailand. After breakfast I wandered down the street and called into the Intercontinental and the Grand Hyatt both within five minutes of the Four Seasons. These are all amazing hotels, with enormous and glamorous lobbies and lots of shops for those who don't like to step outside the hotel. The Grand Hyatt is a very post-modern grandiloquent building full of huge pillars and classical pediments. Inside there are gushing fountains everywhere and large trees. The floor is cool state with marble staircases. The Intercontinental, by contrast, is luxurious and carpeted, with gold and glass. The windows let in the light from the road and the atrium soars up three or four stories. I am not sure the UK has such amazing hotels. They seem to be one of the splendours of Asia and of course they require vast amounts of space, energy and cheap labour for them to become such splendid places to explore and inhabit for a few days.

The temples were buildings designed to astound, amaze, stupefy the worshippers with gold ornaments, fine art, luscious gardens and shady terraces. They are both appealing, open and also slightly aloof. The hotels of Bangkok have taken over the aesthetic of the Thai temples and have continued the dream with different materials and resources. It is strange that Buddhism should have spawned such outrageous exuberance and display. The culture perhaps demanded it and the culture now puts the same effort and drama into hotels and shopping centres as it once invested in monasteries and temples. The temples cannot compete with the hotels for glamour, for welcome or for a seductive taste of paradise. I am not sure Buddha would have approved.

I also had time to visit two amazing shopping centres close by the hotel. I had not bothered to wander into these places before. One is called Zen or the Central Point and has an Isetan department store as its anchor tenant. This building brings all the glamour and abundance of a Japanese department store to down town Bangkok. It is very beautiful and as in Japanese department stores the top floor is full of easy places to eat. I must investigate when I return to Bangkok.

The other store across the way seemed like an enormous hypermarket which had extended into a department store. It was also good but nowhere near as glamorous as Isetan. These places are the pinnacle of Bangkok retailing whereas the street outside Asok which I visited last night occupies the lowest end of the tourism spectrum. The lowest order of the domestic spectrum is probably far from the centre of Bangkok and is pretty poor. This is a country of vast inequality although the young people seem to migrate between these different worlds and presiding over all this mayhem is the urbane and slightly befuddled picture of the King in very large spectacles and perhaps his wife, a portly lady.

Phnom Penh (must check out the spelling) later in the evening

Now this is a really strange and weird place. It is filling me with huge and confused impressions and I can't make out what they all mean.

It was easy to get into the country. Rachel had suggested an e-visa and it all seemed to work really well. I was only queuing for a few minutes, unlike Bangkok which has no travel restrictions for the UK and still it takes thirty minutes to clear immigration. Here I passed across my e-visa and waited. They took finger prints from both hands using a scanning device as well as a picture, I think. They must be worried.

I changed some money after immigration. Since the hotels and others want to be paid in local currency I changed $500 and I got in return 1.85 million something. That is a lot of something. The largest note is 10000. It needed two large envelopes. So almost 4000 things to the dollar. This is going to become very confusing but the shops and hotels etc. are asking for everything in dollars.

I went out for dinner this evening and found a very Indo-Chinese restaurant called the Le Wok. It was a lovely meal served delightfully by very gracious and beautiful people. It took me a while to understand that we did not understand one another because we were all so happy and smiling. The bill came in dollars and I asked if they wanted dollars or the local currency. This question was far too complicated and I gave up very quickly and brought out dollars. We will see what happens.

The hotel sent a driver to the airport for me. This was a luxury which Cornelia would have approved of. It was nice to be collected. He did not speak any English either but it was fascinating to drive with him back into town. There were more bicycles and motor cycles on the streets than in Myanmar or Thailand. The place was far gentler and less wound up than Thailand. It took me a while to spot a monk whereas in Myanmar and Thailand there are plenty of monks. The streets seemed to be well laid out but dirty and yet this was not dusty sandy dirt like Myanmar but something like a post-soviet malaise, if there is such a thing, mixed with a healthy dose of Indian industrial dirt. The people seemed if anything happier and more at ease than those in Thailand and Myanmar. The Thai people are frenetic and stylish. The Cambodians are stylish, wonderfully so and even more beautiful than the Thais but do not seem as driven or as wound up as the Thais. Over the years Thailand has become the new Singapore.

I could not believe how the temperature had dropped when I got off the plane and the skies seemed cloudy and overcast. Later while I was walking around rain started. I found this hard to believe for a moment or two. Surely this could not be rain. I thought this whole region did not get rain until the start of the monsoon season later in the summer. But this was rain, a real tropical downpour, as you get in Singapore. It lasted ten or fifteen minutes and then the rain stopped. After the last few weeks of searing heat the rain was good. However, now that it has passed the humidity is even higher than it was in Thailand or Myanmar. In both these places the heat from 1100 to 1500 is intense and then by 1530 the weather is balmy. This evening it is coolish but with lots of humidity. This is a new climate and a new place full of mysteries.

The hotel is pretty grotty but quite acceptable for a night or two and the manager has gone out of his way to be helpful. He is a young Indian man who dresses smartly in a pink shirt. The staff are all full of smiles and although they seemed to have misunderstood each item of my stay we got it all sorted out in the end. If all goes well I am here for two nights and I will leave on Thursday morning by boat for Siem Reap. This seems a bit of a pipe dream at the moment but I am sure things will sort themselves out by tomorrow. I could not find any way of booking this boat online. The manager is helping me and if he has not managed to do anything by lunch time tomorrow I will try to visit the boat office.

Although the hotel is pretty grotty and the area of town feels straight out of western movie, with many very louche characters, Asian and western, hanging around so chilled that they look as if they have been lounging for the last five years or so, very, very cheap bars and other places offering blind massages etc., when I started walking I found it is very close to the national museum and the royal palace. On the map it looks as if these sights are a good distance away but something magical has occurred and they are just around the corner and the restaurant I found is across from the national museum. I was tempted to think I should go back to the same restaurant tomorrow night but there is another place also around the corner which is run on the same model as Jamie Oliver's restaurant giving young people a chance to work in a restaurant and learn the trade. It looks good and I may be tempted.

The museum looks amazing—wooden and stone construction in bright red wood and stone.

The palace looks amazing—I am not sure if it is open. It looks similar to the buildings in Bangkok. I found from the guide that for Cambodia at least for a significant time, the baddies are the Thais. They come conquer and destroy Phnom Penh. I need to read more.

The silver pagoda may be close to the palace and I should be able to see all of these things tomorrow without much harassment.

The wifi works. Email works (unlike Burma), the air conditioning works. The room and hotel are a bit sleazy but I am only here for a few nights.

I have found a lovely place to eat.

The people are even more charming and beautiful than the Thais.

I thought that the Burmese would add something even sweeter to Buddhism than the Thais but that is not what I found. But here in

Cambodia I have already found something very sweet and endearing in the statues and people.

It is not a paradise because it is so dirty, seedy and confused and yet these things are more than offset by a real and meaningful exoticism. Said would no doubt disapprove but I am captivated. The exotic is the other turned into a source of delight and fascination, even if infantilised.

In Myanmar we always felt that the people were worried that if they did anything bad to tourists, like the monks who objected to how tourists were abusing the monuments and the Buddhas, they would be punished. They were living under a threat. I don't have any sense of a regime here at all. This feels like a raw jungle and on the streets it feels like one. And yet the jungle seems friendly.

The royal palace, museum and the hotel are across from the river. I was walking along the coastal road at sundown. This was very enchanting. Old Chinese style boats with wooden roofs and carved eaves were rushing along the beautiful river, already lit up. It was truly enchanting. The people were promenading and some were making offerings of lotus seed heads to the idols. Cornelia and I were talking about these lotus seed heads in Inle Lake because Inle lake had lots of water lilies but no lotus blooms and it is the lotus which is a Buddhist symbol not the water lily.

Cambodia is a surprise, very different from Myanmar and Thailand, not Chinese. The people are different racially and there is a different mixture of ethnic races. This is a post French colony not a post British colony. And at this stage it is just a series of unanswered questions, a field of impressions demanding some response before the impressions are deadened by becoming familiar. I am glad to be here.

Lazy Traveller Blog 21

21st March 2012, Riverside Hotel in Phnom Penh

In Thailand I have been writing this blog in a Starbucks around the corner from the Four Seasons. It seemed an easy-going place to sit for a while and write. This is the day for Phnom Penh, although I still have not learnt how to spell the city's name. I have looked at it a few times and thought the spelling was obvious but then it disappears from my mind when I start to type it.

Phnom Penh is a hot and sticky city, sleazy and dirty, a city of hustlers, stray bohemian foreigners who look a little lost and determined locals who know the price of everything in dollars. It feels like a hard city in which to survive. And yet it is also a friendly place with lots of people doing their best and going out of their way to be kind to the silly foreigners who stray into their space. I was unsure if I could find anything to enjoy and be surprised by in the city but I have had a good day.

155

I am due to leave tomorrow to head up river to the town of Siem Reap which is the base for visiting Angkor Wat. I asked the hotel to book the boat trip for me but they were struggling. I decided to head off this morning after breakfast to find the jetty from which this fast boat leaves and get this whole thing sorted out at the beginning of the day. I could have flown straight into Siem Reap and missed out on Phnom Penh but I was curious. This is my time to visit this part of the world.

I found the jetty easily enough. I was going to hire a tuk tuk but it took too long to arrange a price and the sun was not high at that time of the morning and I was keen to wander. It is further along the river from the hotel along the river bank. It was good to see the city opening for business. It was good to walk along the river bank.

I found a man who was very willing to sell me a ticket for the boat but since it was now 0715 and the boat should leave daily at 0730 I wanted to see the boat before I made a booking. Eventually it transpired that the boat did not go today because this is the dry season and the river is not high enough. I am not sure what to believe. I saw the fast boat at the jetty. There was no one around and the boat was not moving. This was confirmed by a travel agent whose office I walked into. The young woman there very helpfully made a call and confirmed that the boat did not run today but she could sell me a ticket for the bus which would leave tomorrow at 0730. it would take the same amount of time, around six hours, the bus was air conditioned and the ticket was only $11. I thought I needed to give up on the idea of the boat but since I had left the hotel to arrange things I said I would check with the hotel before I booked a ticket for tomorrow. This whole thing turned into a pleasant surprise. It was far easier to sort out than I expected although I did not end up doing what I had intended. When I talked to the hotel later they were very happy to sell me a ticket for the boat for tomorrow and a return ticket on Sunday. They said two of their guests had departed on the boat this morning! Wow! Now that was a surprise. I decided to give up on the boat and go for the bus. The hotel was happy to arrange and issue the ticket immediately although this time it had dropped in price and was now only $6.50. There will be a small bus which collects me from the hotel at 0630 and the bus will leave Phnom Penh at 0700 fingers crossed, tomorrow morning. I am slightly worried but these things usually work out ok and the hotel is not full. I think I will get to Siem Reap tomorrow by lunch time.

On the way back to the hotel I found a local market and wandered around looking for thing that were different from the markets we visited in Myanmar. The big difference was something that looked religious. Lotus seed ponds were attached to a long bamboo cane stick and people were wandering around with these things which looked like magical wands. I am not sure what they are but I have not seen them before. No doubt I will find someone to ask about them. The market was smaller and even dirtier than the ones we visited in Myanmar.

The next big wonderful surprise was the National Museum which is only a few streets away from the hotel, built in probably an old Khmer style. The building with red wooden columns, red-tiled roof and wooden carved eaves is probably what the Palace in Mandalay should have looked like if the regime had not chosen to rebuild it in concrete and corrugate iron and paint everything red. The Palace was incongruous and strange, eerie and lifeless whereas this museum was one of the best I have visited on this trip. It was an open structure around a courtyard which had lotus blossom pools around a central pavilion holding a Buddha and more goldfish. The gardens were lovely and each of the four sides of the courtyard contained different Khmer treasures.

What was also surprising here is that the Buddhas had a knowing and pleasant smile on their faces. They were more relaxed Buddhas, less ascetic and less troubled. They were more at ease with the country in which they appeared. The Buddha sat beside other Hindu gods (Vishnu, Siva, Krishna etc.), figures from the Cambodia Ramayana and female figures. In Thailand and Myanmar there had been no significant sculptures featuring women, beauty and fertility—all of these concepts had to be conveyed, somewhat stodgily through the figure of the Buddha. Suddenly women were back in the picture and the women were represented as luscious, feminine, very curvaceous and very happy. The sculptures gave a sense of a more inclusive and accepting culture, more open to external influences from India and China and able to digest these influences. Sadly no photos were allowed inside the museum which seemed strange. Photographs are not going to hurt these stone figures.

The stone figures were life size images of human beauty and radiance. It was interesting to look at the stillness, radiance and coherence of the stone figures and compare them with the visitors and the curators. The statues were still radiant idealisations of the human, a long way from the real mess which was represented by the visitors.

Unlike any other museum I have been in, in addition to room guardians who were there to stop visitors from touching the objects, defacing them or taking them away, in this museum there were also ladies offering sweet smelling garlands of jasmine and joss sticks so that you could make an offering and bless the Buddha, thank him for the experience and his teaching. Not every statue was selected for this treatment but there was probably two or three in each of the major rooms. I liked it. it seemed to acknowledge the role these sculptures have in cult worship. Primarily they are not objects in a museum. They are part of the religious tradition of the country. I took my garland and wandered around deciding which image I wanted to give it to. The Museum was a big hit and a wonderful surprise.

The Royal Palace was closed but next to it the Silver Pagoda was open but seemed to be a simple but not very good copy of the Thai Royal Palace and temple. The building style was the same and the main chamber contained an image of the Emerald Buddha, similar to the main treasure in the Royal Palace in Bangkok but there were no murals painted on the walls of the main audience chamber and the murals on the outer cloister had not been restored and were very patchy. I kept asking people for the Silver Pagoda expecting something else but a few people told me that this was the silver pagoda. It was not silver and it was no pagoda. Apparently the floor is made of silver or mirrored tiles but since the floor was covered in rugs this was not visible. The chamber also contained a lot of cultic objects associated with the adoration of the Buddha and crowning of the Kings of Cambodia but none of them seemed to have the beauty and quiet dignity of those images in the Museum. The Palace was underwhelming.

Around the Palace were nice streets of shops and this district was considerably better than the one with the hotel and the ones I travelled through on the way from the airport. On one road junction there was the building of the World Bank.

The last surprise of the morning was the Foreign Correspondent Club. Others had told me to visit and I had forgotten about it but then I stumbled on it around lunch time and had a delicious meal of roast pork on a sesame seed salad with delicious ice cream. The tables on the first-floor veranda looked up and down the river and I was able to sit, eat, relax and read while the sun was at its hottest. The food was delicious and it was good to look at people coming and going for an hour or so.

The heat has now subsided and it is possible to go wandering again, to visit the Central Market and the big pagoda and stupa in the centre of town and find somewhere nice to eat.

I have enjoyed the time in Phnom Penh.

Lazy Traveller Blog 22

22nd March 2012, Phnom Penh to Siem Reap, Babel Guesthouse

I have arrived in Siem Reap and all is well. I have checked in to a small guesthouse I found on line. I was worried that it is very cheap but the staff are very friendly indeed and no doubt the money saved on the room can be spent on incidentals. I asked for a double room and the receptionist was very keen to tell me that the bed was very big. And it is. It is just fine. I think the window looks out onto a wall but that is ok because I did not come here for the view. In a hotel in Hangzhou in China I found there was no window at all in the room. There are no planning restrictions yet in China to say that all rooms should have natural daylight and windows. The hotel was next to the West Lake and it was fine. I think this one will be fine too.

Gabi in Zurich used to differentiate her travels. If she were travelling with someone else she said she was on vacation. But if she were travelling on her own she was on a journey of exploration of some sort. I realise I started on an adventure, was on vacation while Cornelia and I were travelling together and I have returned now to being on an adventure. Myanmar was done as a vacation. Thailand and Cambodia are adventures. And travelling by ordinary bus is always an adventure.

The bus left Phnom Penh at 0700. I was picked by a small hotel at 0630. I came down around 0600 to clear my account and to have breakfast. Everything worked out just fine. The people in all of these places are very friendly although their English skills are barely passable. They struggle to understand but no matter. The hotel in Phnom Penh arranged the bus for me and everything worked out just fine. The small bus took those of us the driver collected from different hotels to the main bus station. I ended up on what I thought was the bus to Siem Riep in seat number 12 in this case, not seat 61, and luggage stowed. I felt well pleased. Someone came around to take the ticket stub and then he came back five minutes later to tell me I was on the wrong bus. I got on the bus the driver of the first pick up had pointed out to me. He had disappeared. I got off the bus sharpish, retrieved by luggage and found the right bus. Then all was well.

The journey took six hours but it takes the same on the river as on the road. This bus was more comfortable than the long boat journey we did from Mandalay to Bagan. The bus was air conditioned. It stopped for a major lunch stop once. It stopped once for a toiler break in the middle of the countryside and everyone dashed off, the men headed in one direction and the women in another. On the way we dropped off some consignments of mangos and other mail which the driver and his mate was commissioned to deliver. At one point three older ladies got on with enormous plants. There were no seats for them for a while but three small stools were produced by the driver and they sat in the gangway until seats became free. I had forgotten how easy long distance bus rides can be abroad. I used these buses a lot to get around Turkey. The ticket always included a numbered seat and a ticket. I never got lost. In Turkey on the system they ensured men were not sitting next to women they did not know.

This bus was very friendly and everyone enjoyed the DVDs, which started off with an hour's karaoke to gentle Cambodian classics. I looked up from time to time and everyone was singing along. We had a kung fu thriller which seemed to revolve around magic and sinister chopsticks and then there was a long romance for a young girl between two men, one had a motor bike and the other had a car.

I arrived safely and well. The hotel said they had sent a tuk tuk driver with a sign but I could not see him. instead one of the bus guards said he was also a tuk tuk driver and he would drop me to my hotel for $1—deal done. He is coming back tomorrow to collect me at 0500 for seven hours of sightseeing for $15. I want to start early, see as much as possible and be back in town and in comfortable shade before the burning time of the day. It is so hot that it is no pleasure to be out between 1200 and 1600.

This evening the hotel has arranged a sunset ride for $5 leaving at 1630. I have no idea what it is going to be like but sometimes it helps to be lazy and just say yes. I am here in Siem Reap until Sunday morning. The hotel will arrange to get me back to a bus station nice and early on Sunday.

In some ways Angkor Wat may be the highlight of this whole tour. It may be the most splendid monument I have visited on this trip: it is a world heritage site. But I am not yet prepared for what I am going to see. Apart from a brief sense of what Khmer art was like at the Museum yesterday in Phnom Penh and looking at the models of Angkor Wat which were part of the royal palaces in Bangkok and Pnom Penh I have no idea what I am going to see and how it will touch me, if at all. It is all very exciting. By sheer chance this major monument has been left to the end. After this visit to Siem Reap I am retracing my steps via first Phnom Penh and then Bangkok before I return to the UK. This is the furthest point out on the journey and it is one of the hottest. I have time before tomorrow at 0500 to read up on Ankgor Wat and to learn a lot very quickly. This is required of a lazy traveller.

The bus was a nice long journey and gave me time to finish *The Glass Palace* by Amitav Ghosh. Cornelia had downloaded it while we were in Myanmar but I picked up a copy as we left Yangon. I have been reading it since then. It is a fascinating book about:

A family over three generations

The arrival and departure of the British, the Japanese and local governance in Burma

The strains within the Indian Army brought about by the Second World War

The disruption pain and loss the Second World War brought about in Burma and Malaysia.

Racism within the British empire

The timber industry in Burma and how it used elephants and Indian slave labour

The exile of the last Burmese King and Queen to India

The Indian economic diaspora

The growing sense of the necessity of Indian independence and home rule

In some ways this is fictional account not unlike the *Hare with Amber Eyes* which charts a family spread out across Europe and the Middle East through the 20th century. The family in this case is Burmese and Indian and suffers the glories and the vicissitudes of the 20th century. It is a fascinating insight into so much of Burma and it is a great book to read for background. It captures a lot of the bigger narratives which Myanmar has been involved in.

It is not necessarily a great novel. It is weak in texture and the characterisation is poor (except for 1. mother and child issues, which are done well and 2. a long theme on the subject of loyalty and betrayal suffered by the Indian Army as the Empire comes to an end. The story focuses on an Indian battalion of the British Army before the end of the Empire. This theme culminates in the terrible execution by an Indian officer of the Indian batman and villager who has served as a symbol of the virtue of Indian loyalty throughout the novel).

The book seems to have been written with the eye on a film adaptation. But it is very good and I have enjoyed reading it over the last few days. It is put into the shade by *The Hare with Amber Eyes* which is narrated so skilfully and so artfully and *A Suitable Boy* by Vikram Seth which is such a tour de force of narration and style.

As at the end of any long novel I have a sense of disappointment now that the journey is over. I wanted to stay longer in this world with these characters and find out more.

Lazy Traveller Blog 23

23rd March 2012, Siem Reap, Babel Guesthouse

I was up this morning at 0430 and the tuk tuk driver arrived at 0500 so that I could be at Angkor Wat for sunrise. I have had a great day wandering around the monuments which started yesterday evening with a trip to the monument at sunset.

But before the monuments there are other surprises.

The guesthouse is very sweet but the staff are kind and very helpful. The guesthouse is owned by a Norwegian and a Swedish couple and they have been allowed to run it for five years, on a lease, I suppose. This is the fourth year. The guesthouse seems to have a posse of tuk tuk drivers attached to it. These are some of the nicest tuk tuk drivers I have come across. The man who drove me yesterday spoke very well and told me a lot about Siem Reap and the monuments in very good English. I was surprised at his fluency in comparison with the people we met in Burma.

Cambodia may be as poor as Myanmar—if anything it may be poorer and yet the culture is very different, despite the Cambodia war and the Pol Pot regime. In Phnom Penh the drivers wanted to take me to the killing fields and the assassination camps but I opted out of these sights. I know what I cannot take. I am happy to read the stories. I don't think I need to see these places of evil. It is assumed as a tourist you are willing and keen to see these sights but I am not sure why. It is one thing to visit something which represents a pinnacle of human culture and development in some way. Killing fields, extermination camps and assassination camps don't have the same fascination and attraction. I am not sure I could cope with them emotionally, especially when I am travelling on my own.

So the guesthouse is a pleasant surprise and the tuk tuk drivers very helpful and supportive. I did not expect a guesthouse to have a group of helpful drivers. In Bagan even when we asked for a guide and driver we were provided with a pair whose English was not even passable. When I came back from the long sightseeing trip this morning the guesthouse managed to serve pancakes and coffee—this was a lovely and simple surprise. I did not feel like breakfast at 0500 and for the rest of the morning I was keen to keep moving from monument to monument before the heat became prohibitive.

A slightly more surprising thing happened this morning on the drive to Angkor Wat. I noticed on the pavement on a big open green space a large number of people sleeping or resting. This was still very early. As we continued to drive past I realised this was the local children's' hospital and there was a huge sign outside the hospital saying there was a huge danger of dengue fever and the hospital was clearly on red alert. I am not sure I know what Dengue fever is but I think this was a children's hospital and I think all the people waiting outside were the parents of the children being treated inside the hospital. I am not sure about any of this. I am reminded of Eschenbach in *Death in Venice*; he notices the city is changing as a result of cholera. The disease is arriving in Venice and the city will become closed before Eschenbach tries to leave. He drinks a glass of contaminated water and he dies in what has become a troubled image of paradise and hell. I don't mean to be melodramatic but the huge queues outside the hotel both here and in Phnom Penh are worrying. Behind the Royal Palace in Phnom Penh I was surprised to see the same signs outside a hotel I stumbled upon. Something is clearly going on. No one has talked about this outbreak – but that is what happens in *Death in Venice* too. I hope all is well and there is no great danger to the local children and their parents and I hope that I will be able to leave Siem Reap as planned on Sunday and leave for Bangkok on Monday.

Last night I had a tuk tuk who drove me to Angkor Wat for sunset. We paused on the way for me to buy a ticket for three days. The ticketing is all done very professionally and I assume the money goes back into supporting the local efforts to continue to investigate the monuments. There are a lot of them, as in Bagan. At the ticket office they have cameras, as they do now at all the immigration desks at airports and the photo they take there and then goes onto your ticket which is inspected each time you try to enter any monument around the city.

It was great to visit the monument last night and this morning. This is the main monument but there are many others. This main monument is a temple mountain, a temple like structure which represents the Hindu view of the universe. You come into the monument along a huge path with carved snakes along its edges and you cross a huge moat which surrounds the whole temple complex and represents the oceans of the world. Each element of the monument is a microcosm of the whole and replicates the same structure. We have seen this same principle of micro and macrocosm in Ayutthaya where the tiny gold reliquary buried deep within the stupa at the heart of the city temple was itself a model of the whole stupa. In the case of Angkor Wat, the overall shape is a square containing two symmetrical and paired libraries leading to an inner courtyard which contains the same thin and then at the heart is a mountain complex which represents the five sacred mountains of the Hindu world.

This complex structure is new for me on this trip. This is also not a religious monument per se. It honours a powerful king of Khmer who fought many battles and ruled a large kingdom. This is his mausoleum and celebrates his successes and the gods who had taken care of him. In the Buddhist temples we visited you generally visit the temple in a clockwise direction. Here direction is reversed—perhaps to indicate that this is not sacred history but secular history. This is a king so powerful that he builds a temple to celebrate his own achievements and the monument is in stone, whereas we are told that only gods live in stone houses in Cambodia. The people including the royal family lived in wooden structures, raised platform houses on stilts and these are the sort of houses which are still visible on the long road from Phnom Penh to Siem Reap. The style has not changed in the 20th century but now the new houses are built on concrete not wooden poles and the wooden poles plus reinforced concrete can carry bigger weight and so the houses are larger.

The temple at Angkor is celebrated for its wall bas reliefs which are built into the walls all around the outer perimeter of the monument. It takes a long time to look at these walls reliefs. They are mainly now in a good state. They tell tales of war, featuring elephants and warriors. On certain walls they represent the virtues on the upper level and vices on the lower levels. On other walls stories of the Ramayana are included. This is an exception since the Ramayana tells the stories of Rama and Sita (his wife). For the most part the bas reliefs mainly depict warriors and men in battle whereas the sections surrounding the bas reliefs and the area around all the doors and gates feature beautiful large breasted Cambodian dancing girls. These are beautiful stone carvings. Women are dancing girls and very beautiful (or apsara, heavenly nymphs), the men are warriors and ride elephants to war: that is the general story which comes across.

This monument was made even more beautiful by the use of water. The monument floats on the ocean of the world represented by the moat. And then inside the monument, at every level there are further lakes or pools; the right-hand side always a direct reflection of the left. This is an ordered, patterned and symmetrical world. These pools must have been beautiful when the monument was at its peak. This morning, at sunrise I found one of the pools on the left-hand side was partly filled with blooming red-pink water lilies. They were too small to feature in the pictures but they were there.

These elements are all surprising: focus on a king and his successes; bas reliefs, external moat and pools, mountain complex, amazing turned windows, moving around the complex anticlockwise, the monument goes west to east, in distinction to temples which go from east to west, "libraries" (this is what these small internal structures are called. I assume they contained the written records on wood or stone which document the stories and facts of the king's successes). And a big surprise is that although Cambodia now is a Buddhist country this is not a Buddhist monument. This is a Hindu structure celebrating the male Hindu gods, Shiva.

These gods are quite different from the Buddha and they represent powerful mythical human powers—life and destruction, the will to power, sameness and difference. It is hard to change my mind to Hindu issues after so much Buddhism. Even in the national museum in Phnom Penh the Buddhas are the figures which are celebrated with incense and flower garlands. There is an attempt here to replace the Hindu figures with Buddhist interpretations of the same animal, e.g. the snake and the elephant.

One wonderful surprise yesterday evening was when I got to the central stupa complex representing the five sacred mountains of the world, as the sun was beginning to set the birds began to sing. These were wonderful birds and the sound was haunting.

This morning I arrived at this section of the complex after sunrise but the sun was still rising on the horizon beyond the monument. The sun rose through the far eastern windows of the complex.

Originally there was a golden Hindu idol (of Vishnu) at the top of the sacred mountain. This has now gone. It was replaced by four figures of Buddha looking out at the different cardinal points of the compass; these have also gone and so the monument becomes a simple pyramid, connecting this tower of Babel, (a recurring motif of all ancient sacred and heroic builders), with the pyramids in Egypt and the huge pyramids in Mexico City and Chichen Itza. This monument is built around four central directions and a central point—the quincunx motif. This great Khmer king symbolically and through his battles triumphed over the four corners of the world and turned this place into the centre of the world, the place which linked the heavens and the earth, time past with time present and time future. This sacred mountain pulled together the power of man with the power of the gods. The gods' presence prove that this king is blessed and his triumphs involve an unfolding of some divine plan. It was not just the British empire which had such beliefs in itself and its own god-given right to rule over its vassal states.

It was great to have time to wander around the monument last night and it was good to go back this morning in the dark and then wander around in the cool of the morning.

There are many other temples and monuments. More to write about tomorrow.

While I have been writing under the rush matting roof of the guesthouse bar there has been a rain storm and so now the place is cooler suddenly but more humid. We are in the jungle and this is what it feels like.

Lazy Traveller Blog 24

24th March 2012, Siem Reap, Babel Guesthouse

I am having a quiet day. Or at least that is the plan. I am travelling back to Phnom Penh tomorrow and I should leave the guesthouse at 0615. The return journey should take six hours or so and it would be good to get it over early in the day on an air-conditioned bus.

People from the guesthouse have just left for a day trip to visit a famous temple on the border of Cambodia and Thailand. They were due to leave around 0700 but they have just left at 0800. The journey to the mountain is going to take them four hours. They will then climb the mountain to the temple for an hour or so and then return. They will probably return by 8pm this evening. They asked me if I wanted to join them. I had no interest, I am afraid. My stomach is playing up a bit and this is an ideal day to rest before the journey back to Phnom Penh and Bangkok. I realise that I am no longer a traveller.

The visit to Angkor Wat yesterday morning was a great moment and it has taken a while to digest the meaning of this place because it seems so different from other monuments we have visited. In Myanmar the focus was on Buddhism and in Thailand royalty and so the state is celebrated through Buddhism as well. And Buddhism leads to a loss of personality. The heroic is subsumed into the consciousness of the Buddha and clearly Buddha has no time for battles, victories and nation building. That is partly why Buddhism is not leading to social change in Myanmar still. It leads to a sort of quietism and a lack of interest in action. Angkor Wat was built and arises from a complete different conception of kingship, nation hood and personality. It is built by, or in commemoration of, Suryavaman II, 1112-1152. He is a warrior king and he celebrates the Hindu god Vishnu, the king's tutelary god. This is a celebration of a king's achievements in war against his enemies and those attempting to conquer the kingdom. And Vishnu is the ideal projection for the kingly and state building characteristics of such a king.

Before I left the UK I was reading Shakespeare's first tetralogy on the wars of the roses, i.e. Henry VI, 2,3 and 1 and then Richard III. In the background of these plays looms the figure of Henry V, who is clearly the warrior king, like Edward III, who is the British equivalent warrior king of England. We are in the same space. Henry VII as the king who ends the War of the Roses builds the Henry VII chapel at Westminster as a fitting burial place for himself and to promulgate the values of chivalry he believed in as a Christian king. Suryavaman II is doing something similar in Angkor Wat but it is clear that this kingdom of Cambodia has immense resources to call upon, to build and irrigate such a temple in the middle of the tropical forest. It must have taken huge engineering capability, financial resources and human resources to build such a colossal monument, which rivals the great pyramids in Egypt (built for similar reasons to glorify kings with long and successful reigns) and the Mayan and Aztec temples in Mexico. All of these show great confidence and the kings had rich domains which could produce the additional wealth required to build such amazing monuments.

Shakespeare is writing his plays after the event and he is not in the service of one of the monarchs he represents. His plays are based on a completely different view of history and kingship. He still remains close to us in the way he depicts power, subterfuge, civil war and the huge difficulty of bringing social order out of a chaos brought about by warring individuals competing for self-interest, disguised as loyalty to the crown. In many ways Shakespeare remains a contemporary whereas Angkor Wat is an exotic but closed mystery. Now it is just a ruin. To get any real grasp of its meaning and its splendour we would need to see it inhabited with the different spaces occupied. It is like visiting the Forbidden City versus watching Bertolucci's *Last Emperor*. The latter brings Chinese imperial court to life in a way that Shakespeare brings to life the Wars of the Roses. Visiting the ruins in Siem Reap leave me hungry to know more. The ruins evoke a hunger which they don't satisfy although they give us a great sense of the exotic and the huge power this country once had. Ozymandias comes to mind again and the multiple copies of the heads on the Bayon could be Ozymandias himself.

Siem Reap is like Bagan. It has multiple monuments which were built over a period of 200 or 300 years. It is impossible to see all of them and Khmer fatigue comes into play. The short circuit, which was one I did yesterday, takes in a number of the large and imposing monuments and these were wonderful. I was using the guidebook leant me by Tim and Reid and their copy includes their detailed itinerary for the dates when they were here in November a few years ago. I ended up seeing similar things. I managed to see Angor Wat, Angkor Thom, Bayon (city temple with heads), Baphuon (sacred hill), the royal palace (now derelict but has pools and sweet ladies having a picnic and other men watering the gardens), Phimeanakas, Preah Pralilay (boy learning Japanese), Tep Pranam, elephant terrace and terrace of leper king, city gates and brides, Ta Keo, Ta Nei, To Prohm (jungle has taken over the temple and the trees are now surplanting the monuments, strange and surreal but very busy when I was there and it was very hot).

Angkor Wat is a temple dedicated to one king whereas Angkor Thom is the city that was built after Angkor Wat; built and rebuilt as a result of invasions and power moving away from and then back to the Khmer regimes. Bayon is the city temple at the heart of the city and so similar to the temple I visited in Ayutthaya which formed the mythological heart of the city and connected the upper worlds with the mundane world of the city. In that case the city was dedicated to Buddha and so the central stupa contained relics of the body so that celestial and eternal power would be present and radiate out of the city's centre. Angkor Thom is dedicated to Avalokiteshvara—I am not clear who this is but what remains now is an enigmatic human face. It does not look like a Buddha and it does not like look a Hindu god. It is Big Brother, an idealised, smiling, beneficent but strong, probably male character. This is an embodiment of the super ego of the state. It is an idealised figure of the state, the ancestors, the dead and the living—the figure is not old but at the height of its power. It is not necessarily a contemplative figure like the

Buddha. It is contented not merely with interiority and consciousness but with what exists in the world. It is a city which believes in its own immense power of creativity and innovation and resilience. This city will survive, the god tells us (although it did not). It is a projection of human potency actualised in the city rather than a particular king. It is the will, the life force, perhaps the spirit of the Khmer themselves.

And the temple has many, many such images. The architectural innovation seems to be to give the same stone blocks usually making up a stone mountain or a stupa a human face and then replicate the face a thousand-fold, in the same way that the Buddha's image is replicated many times in Buddhist temples.

This temple is at heart of the city and then there are monuments around the city.

Although the monuments were interesting and fascinating what surprised me were two incidents involving people. In one abandoned temple there was a young boy around 14 who was hanging around offering information as a guide and hoping for an offering from tourists. I sat for a while and talked with him, because it was getting hot and I needed to catch up on the guidebook. I was getting confused between elephant terraces, temples, pools and leper terraces. He wanted to practice his Japanese phrases. This was quite fun. He had a Japanese teacher at school. He showed me a class picture of the young Japanese teacher and his school mates. The Japanese teacher had given them a series of phrases. It was fascinating to go through them with him and find the answers. I have not spoken Japanese for years. This was fun.

It was as if he came from *Le Petit Prince* and he inhabited this temple as characters in that book occupy their own planets which the little prince visits. He was the 14-year-old boy who was learning Japanese in his summer vacation.

As I was walking away from this temple I heard someone chanting very vigorously. I walked towards the sound. The guidebook said that Buddhist nuns occupied one of these temples but the sound did not sound like Buddhist nuns. I found the chanter. He was a young monk who was chanting ferociously and vigorously as he doused someone with water. The man he was dousing was sitting in a prayerful attitude as the monk chanted over him and poured container after container over his head. This went on for about five minutes. I have never seen this ritual before. This whole area of South East Asia is very focused on water and many of the religious rituals are based on water. I had not seen a religious wash in public before. It was fascinating. The man who had been doused was replaced by his wife. The monk took a breather and returned. The buckets of water he used for the ritual wash had been replenished by a young boy who was not a monk from a well a few steps away from the monk who was washing the man on the staircase of a prayer hall. This was a big surprise and given the heat it would have been a nice thing to experiment with. But that was not on offer.

Later yesterday evening I wandered into the town of Siem Reap to get something to eat and to visit the local market. There was a modern Buddhist temple just off the central market. The monks were arriving for a chanting session. I have not come across many of these sessions on my travels. We have seen monks walking the streets, monks going out to get the offerings from people in the morning, monks eating, monks sight-seeing. But not many monks chanting with other monks. There was a large temple in Bangkok where I did see this and there was a monk with a very strong voice leading the mesmerising chant. Last night there were only ten monks or so and they took up their positions on the red carpet in front of the main idol. Other local people crept in around the edges and there were some foreigners like me at the back. It was good to sit and enter this mesmerising space of the chant. This is how these places need to be experienced rather than just as a shrine with images and idols. It was interesting to see the monks change their posture after a while and finding a position that was comfortable, always covering their feet since these obviously give a lot of offence. The monks here wear orange-coloured robes.

I entered the market near the fresh fish stall and by that time in the day, around 1700, the smell was overpowering. I had to come out and go back in via a different route. There were stalls selling spices, including bags of amazing-coloured saffron, a special yellow concoction for fish curry, jasmine tea and many others.

I have just come back from the museum. I decided I would venture out and see what this museum had to offer. The man at the desk offered to drive me there and I said yes. He appeared on his motor bike in a helmet and I was to hop on the back. The journey was very short, only five or seven minutes but I realised that this was probably the maddest thing I had done on this journey—not so mad really but a bit stupid. I would not jump on the back of a motorbike in UK without a helmet and here I was speeding along a road in Siem Reap—the wrong way as often on a motorbike clinging on a pillion passenger. I felt really stupid but the journey only lasted a short time and the lazy traveller arrived shaken and stirred by the experience.

The museum is excellent and helped fill in a few missing pieces of the jigsaw. The king who built Angor was clearly a bit of a monomaniac but he prised the country away from Indonesian control, although he spent a fair amount of his youth in Indonesia. He established the cult of his own personality based on Vishnu and Hindu deities. Buddhism may have existed at that stage in the country, as it did in Myanmar but the king did not decide to make it the cornerstone of nation building.

The man who came later and built Anghor Thom clearly had decided to adopt Buddhism as the national religion. The figure of Avalokiteshvara is a bodhisattva, or the face of the king himself. This king (a long name of which he is the seventh) is also a warrior and he secures the nation's borders again and extends them. This is an era of Khmer military triumph but he decides to adopt Buddhism as a national religion and the figure of Avalokiteshvara morphs into his own image but he has transformed himself from a warrior king into a figure of good order, wisdom and compassion.

Later Buddhist kings were clearly embarrassed by Angkor and its aggrandisement of one king and so they transformed it from a Hindu temple and mausoleum focused on the immemorial cult of the dead ancestor into a Buddhist monastery. This Angkor became Angkor Wat (wat = monastery). The place was filled with images of the Buddha and where necessary the iconography of Angkor was subsumed into Buddhism to become part of Khmer mythology. At Angkor some of the faces have been defaced. It must have been hard for the monks to accept the iconography of Hinduism and its cult of the warrior, the triumph of the will, the warrior and the illusions of rule.

Anghor Wat became the spiritual appendage to the civil authority and reality of Anghor Thom, the city. The motif of the battle with the multi-headed primeval water snake between good and evil was carried over to the new city and this battle is enacted on each of the four city bridges giving access to the city gates, looked over by the head of Avalokiteshvara.

Buddhism was accepted as the more intellectual, more noble and more ascetic religion and a better basis for nationality that the cult of kings and Hinduism with its celebration of the life force. Buddhism with its monastic disciplines and its cults was accepted as the basis of national identity. This, in itself, is a big thing to do. This battle for the soul of the nation seems to have been won by Buddhism. The country and the people define themselves as Buddhists and the monks have a role to play in the community, although not in society, as in Myanmar.

The king who adopted Buddhism turned the state into an organ of beneficence, establishing hospitals (for different castes) and hospices for girls with nowhere else to go.

The pretty apsara with their full bare breasts are a remnant of the Hindu phase. Nowadays the women are not bare breasted and it is interesting to see Cambodian national dance. All the roles are played by women, including the warriors, the devils and old men. The dance is very hieratic and focuses on the hands mainly with some minor emphasis on the feet. The helmets the dancers wear are equivalent to stupas, large pinnacles of many tiers. They are very beautiful but have a very stilted and confused sensuality. It is hard to see how such a Buddhist country copes with a tradition of the apsara, which is very close to Hugh Hefner and buxom playboy models. The apsara are not fertility figures. They are serving maidens, they are the fair reward of warriors, they are creatures of pleasure (not necessarily their own).

The museum also confirmed that the only technology used in these temples is the lintel. The arch does not arrive in any of these temples and monuments. Bagan must have got the arch from the Indian architects and engineers. The whole spectacle of Angkor What and the rest of these Khmer monuments are built without recourse to the arch. This society is clearly wealthy enough to afford the vast amount of resources required for these buildings of public spectacles but they are not investing in engineering capability and they are not open to foreign innovation and influences. Eventually as might be expected the Angkor era ended when the country was invaded by foreign invaders, who probably had superior military technology.

Lazy Traveller Blog 25

25th March 2012, Phnom Penh, Riverside Hotel

I am back in Phnom Penh after a long day on the road. But I am back at the small French Cambodian restaurant with the lovely waiting staff for cocktails and some writing time. The vicious heat subsided a few hours ago and now everyone is starting to walk out along the river bank. This is Sunday evening and this is my last night in Cambodia. Tomorrow I leave for Bangkok. This is the beginning of the end of my Cambodia.

Last night I wandered around town to look at the shops and find something nice to eat. Bill says he wants more details of food. I have been feeling a bit queasy for a day or so and I had to give up on everything while I was travelling a lot but last night I went back to a place called the Khmer kitchen. This was a local place across from the market. A young man was grilling chicken at the front as passers-by watched him. But I went instead for Pumpkin and Coconut Soup. And the menu told me that it was filled with coconut cream, long beans, pumpkin, spicy paste, white egg, chilli and tofu. It was like a variation on a Thai soup but with no prawns in this case but lots of very interesting vegetable. It was good.

I wandered across the river to a new section on the market. This is where I saw Cambodian dancing the night before. I tried to get to a performance but I could not manage it but this televised version was good. Last night as I wandered past the same large outdoor screen there was an ABC documentary about Angkor What and the engineering problems which the architects and builders had resolved in building this huge temple complex. This was fascinating, just what I wanted to learn about. We were told of the physical difficulties of placing any large building on such an unstable water table. This had been resolved with the use of the vast moat and the video graphics showed what would happen to the temple without the moat. The temple is built from a local stone called laterite and the experts were explaining how the laterite was ideal for building this sort of weighty mass structure. However, laterite is a very ugly pitted stone to look at and the whole temple is fronted in sandstone which was cut and transported from the north of Cambodia on rafts which are represented on some of the temple buildings. I love this sort of investigative documentary where great academic experts talk about their chosen subject with great lucidity. We were shown how the sandstone was chiselled to form blocks and then levelled out. The whole complex is made without any mortar whatsoever. I had not realised that. The sandstone blocks were rubbed against one another to turn them into fully level surfaces, almost miraculously. There are no joins visible anywhere on the complex. The temple carvings of the bas relief were explained and how they were made by master carvers and apprentices. We also heard that the carved bas relief panels which are on the outside walls of the whole temple complex were completely faced in gold! Some of the gold is still visible. I had no idea of the gilding of the stone bas reliefs. This was a great documentary and was full of surprises. It should have been shown at the Museum which focused on cultural and Buddhist history rather than the building of the monument and how the designers solved a whole series of amazing problems. It was a lucky chance that this documentary was playing as I walked by. There were video shops close by but I could not see if the documentary being shown on the big screen was for sale. This sort of documentary which does not patronise the audience and gives us access to first rate scholarship in an accessible manner is very good. I sat and watched it for a while, being encouraged meanwhile to participate in a fish massage. I declined the fish massage.

My second surprise of the day was the hassle involved in getting back to Phnom Penh. The hotel had arranged a bus ticket for me and they had told me I had to be down in reception by 0615 for a pickup and the bus would leave Siem Reap by 0700. I was still in reception at 0655 and no pickup arrived. I went beyond worry and decided if this bus was not going to happen some other means could be found to get me back to Phnom Penh. I know in the UK if you are not at the right place at the right time for buses and stations all is lost. I got the strong impression that this was not the case in Cambodia. If I had a ticket the bus would wait and would not leave until everyone was on the bus. This is a very different way of working and living; it takes some getting used to but it seems ok.

The pickup bus eventually arrived and I got on with another Dutch lady who is living in Cambodia working on the legal side of the war crimes commission. She was heading to a wedding in the direction of Phnom

Penh. She was going to catch the same bus for half of the way and then change to another bus. The wedding would take place when she arrived. She had become part of the culture and seemed very at ease with the change of timetable. She had an enormous case— gigantic and the young man from my hotel went out of his way not just to help her but to carry it for her. They were good people. while I was waiting at reception I had the time to read more about all the NGOs working around Siem Reap to protect children, deal with the after effect of landmines and train people with new skills. I also read guidelines about not giving money directly to children and not buying things directly from them on the street but it was better to give donations to the formal organisations which are in place to help. The hotel staff had all been trained and graduated from a local hotel school and they are very good.

The bus did not leave eventually until 0800 but I had a seat and once I had been picked up from the hotel and realised that the scrappy piece of paper which the hotel assured me was a ticket was accepted as such by the bus company I stopped worrying. I realised that this journey was going to take a while but all would probably be well. We arrived back in Phnom Penh around 1430 so it was a long journey. The Chinese Cambodian lady behind me went into fog horn mode around 0805 and she continued talking very loudly for the whole journey. I don't know who was the recipient, if anyone, of this long monologue. The woman sitting next to me got her son's mobile phone and decided to see if she could use it as juke box to entertain the whole bus and drown out the Cambodian woman fog horn blast. It was mayhem but we were on the move, on the right bus and heading in the right direction. My stomach was stable. I was happy.

At some stage I gave up on the noise around me and dived into a book and breathed a sigh of relief when the mobile phone was replaced by Cambodian karaoke on the bus's tv system. All things are relative. The bus was fascinating but no one was able to talk to me other than the other foreigners and so this was not a way to get to know Cambodian people but it was a great opportunity for people-watching.

Travelling alone means that I end up with more opportunities for reading and these long journeys on buses seem perfect for long stretches of reading. They are almost as good as a long plane journey. I finished off Karen Armstrong's very good short biography of Buddha. I felt I needed to know more about the man after getting to know his image so well over the last few weeks. The biography was a real surprise. And I started Yann Martel's *Life of Pi*, which I had picked up in Siem Reap. The latter is amazing and tells the story of a young strange boy who grows up in a zoo in Pondicherry and ends up in Canada studying zoology (writing a dissertation on the sloth) and religion (writing about someone obscure). The style, tone and narration are masterly and mysterious. It has been around years but I have not got around to it. I am only fifty pages in but already I am looking forward to returning to it this evening and finding out what happens next. I have no idea what to make of it yet. The prose is dazzling and amusing in a way that Ghosh's *Glass Palace* was not. Ghosh was worthy, a good historical novel and will make a great movie. The Yann Martel is already exciting and very stimulating. I suppose I should add both Armstrong and the *Life of Pi* to the surprises and pleasures of Cambodia along with the Pumpkin and Coconut Soup.

It was a pleasant surprise to return to Phnom Penh. It is only a few days since I left but I was happy to get back this afternoon. I have been on a journey and seen a lot since I left. Phnom Penh is now a city I know. I understood the map better than I did when I last arrived. I have a list of things I want to do and places where I want to sit and dream for a while before I leave tomorrow. I already know the people at the hotel and I knew how to deal with the tuk tuk drivers at the bus station. I am competent again. Arriving at a new place makes me feel very incompetent and so anxious. Arriving somewhere I know brings on no such anxieties. It is good to come back. The familiar is good. I am not sure I am ready to think more generally about Cambodia yet. That may have to wait until tomorrow on the flight back to Bangkok.

The journey to Cambodia is coming to an end and there are now no more new places on the itinerary—no new visas, no new airlines, no new hotels, no new cities. Everything on the rest of the trip is easy. It is nice to relax and wind down a bit more. New places are exhausting and the trip as a whole has been exhausting. Cornelia did all of the planning for Myanmar and yet each place etc. was still exhausting in its own way and we managed the novelty together. I managed Thailand and Cambodia myself. It feels good to be back here tonight in Phnom Penh staying at a hotel I already know. I am having cocktails in a place where I ate before and decided I like. I have been to shops this afternoon which I wanted to go back to. I am having dinner this evening at the Foreign Correspondents Club where I had lunch when I was in Phnom Penh before I left for Siem reap. I feel lazy, contented and relaxed. I don't think I have Dengue Fever and I think I will leave as planned tomorrow afternoon for Bangkok. I am heading home.

When I checked in to the hotel this afternoon they told me they had to upgrade me to a suite because they had a huge party for the next few days. The room I am in is very strange spread on two levels with balconies on both levels. There is a large double bed on both floors and two bathrooms. I go up the top bedroom on a very narrow flight of stairs. I suppose this is a family suite of rooms. I decided I was not going to try to carry my case up that staircase. This is a lot of room for one person but I will only be here one night.

Lazy Traveller Blog 26

26th March 2012, Phnom Penh, Riverside Hotel

I am checked out and ready to head back to the airport for my flight to Bangkok. I have had a good stay in Phnom Penh.

Last night, after cocktails and some time to write, I headed around the corner for dinner at a restaurant which trains young people to run restaurants. All the staff wore the same coloured t-shirts but some carried the word teacher on the back, while others said student. It was a great place. I had a very spicy stir fry with local vegetables and sea food. That was what the menu said and that description corresponds to what appeared but the description does not convey the wonderful flavour, the size and colours of the vegetables and the overall taste. It was delicious. A great end to my eating in Cambodia and a lovely place.

At the table next to me were three young Brits and an American thinking about the night ahead and their plans for the next few days.

Some wanted to travel to Siem Reap to see Angkor Wat and some decided it was too expensive in terms of the travel, an overnight stay and the ticket to the monument. They were on a tight budget. It is good not to be young anymore. Another said he wanted to spend two days in Siem Reap working with an NGO who helps families living on the rubbish mountain of Siem Reap. The volunteers spend time working with the families and getting to know them, helping them with the rubbish sporting. These rubbish mountains are all over the world. This would be a great thing to do. Both hard and difficult. I did not even attempt anything like this but I thought it was a great idea. It was good to hear this chap determined to have a go at doing this.

Dickens features the London rubbish mountains of 19th century London in *Our Mutual Friend*. I am not sure if there is a novelist who has captured the spirit and the flavour of Cambodia. It needs Dickens, Tolstoy, Vikram Seth or the man in Japan who wrote the *The Makioka Sisters*. India is well served by novelists who write in English. Perhaps the Cambodian writers will write in Cambodian or in French. The country needs great imaginative writers who can work in film or the novel to celebrate and bring some understanding to the nation. I am not sure Buddhism does it and the nation's history is so complicated that historians quite rightly will disagree for a long time. The novel remains the perfect form for this narration of the Great Work of a nation and a people. We were fortunate to find such a book in *The Glass Palace* for Myanmar. I need to look around for something similar for Cambodia.

The young people were concerned that they had mobiles which worked before they went out on a drinking spree. This was the key issue. They had to find a way of getting their mobiles to work in Phnom Penh before they would feel safe to go out for the evening. Interesting. Things move on. I have been out of mobile contact with the world for what seems like a long time.

I had a walk around the city along the river and then retired. I found the room although vast was occupied already by many creatures. I wondered for a while if I had left a window open by mistake but I hadn't. It was late and I gave up. But this morning when I woke up there seemed to be a lot of little white ant-looking creatures on the bed and on my netbook. Cornelia and I had a long discussion about bed bugs in New York and she woke me to the dangers of bed bugs. Was this room infested with bed bugs? Cornelia's advice had been that the bed bugs hide in luggage not in people and so it is important not to leave your luggage or a jacket on a bed bug infested bed. This was good advice. I ensured that my suitcase was a good way from the bed. Bed bugs don't jump. I thought I was safe but when I opened my netbook this afternoon at the airport I found quite a few of the little white ants were still around. I did not check with Cornelia what a bed bug looked like. I was too intrigued by the effects the bed bugs had on a friend of hers. In retrospect I am pleased I did not have a second night in the same room. In the smaller room I had slept earlier at the same hotel I had no visitors. The bed bugs or their friends seem to have disappeared from the netbook. I am keen to see if they join me at the Four Seasons in Bangkok.

On the way out of the city a few days ago and on our return yesterday the bus passed a huge tower block that is under construction and close to completion. This is going to be the heart of the developing business world and business district in Phnom Penh. Called Vattanac Towers it is built in the shape of a dragon arising from the waters (or a naga with only one head). Already this tower block dominates the city skyline. The air flight magazine from Bangkok says that Cambodia is about to have huge growth in its economy, partly driven by textiles. This morning, I visited the central market, which is the current local economy. This is an old French early 20th century building. It is painted white and yellow and is in an art deco style. It is amazing and was full. This was a much more well to do market than the ones I visited in Siem Reap. Around the market were clothes shops with branded shirts priced at $250. I am not sure if these prices are for show or if someone is paying these prices. I was surprised by these strange sort of prices and surprised by the market. I picked up some local handicraft items. - strange sense of prices, and Wat Phnom.

The largest Wat or stupa in the city is Wat Phnom and I managed to find it this morning. The city is flat and is built on the banks of the river. I suspect the river rises a lot during the monsoons and I am not sure what happens to the city during the floods. But Wat Phnom is on one of the few high spots in the city. Near the river there is a picture of Phnom Penh from the 1880s; it is an idyllic scene of houses built on stilts on the river bank with the Wat, as it is now, in the background on the small knoll. The Wat has been rebuilt many times. It is not spectacular but it was an interesting place to wander around, my last Cambodian temple for a while. The documentary about Anghor Wat pointed out that the original temples were on mountains because the gods lived in the mountains. This was an animist religion and includes the same sort of mountain worship we find in Japan and in China. The gods lived on high mountains. So Anghor Wat built for a king who made himself a god, featured the great five holy mountains at its centre. And he was buried at the heart of this mountain complex. These temple complexes brought the mountains into cities and into ritual life away from the mountains themselves.

The stupa is another form of the same mountain. When Buddhism comes along the god who is initially buried in the mountain or stupa is the Buddha or a relic of the Buddha. Royal figures had stupas built as a way of becoming in their own way mountain gods, i.e. natural and royal ancestors. And then the stupa becomes the natural form for memorials, graves etc. The stupa and its form of repeats the lingam connecting the female and male, earth and heaven, this time and immortality.

At one side of this stupa was a small girl attempting to delouse the ear of a dog which was ready to give birth. The girl was holding the dog very carefully, perhaps because the dog was troubled by the fleas. The dog yelped from time to time but had a lot of trust in the girl. This was a surprising moment. Karen Armstrong's book talks about the Buddha's discovery of compassion. Chinese Buddhism represents compassion through the figure of Kanon. The Cambodians seem a very compassionate as well as amazingly resilient people but I have seen very few attempts to represent compassion. This young girl delousing the very pregnant dog is my image of compassion from Cambodia. And this form of compassion is in stark contrast to the longing for immortality and grandeur represented by the stupas and temples.

Cornelia had brought with her a bag of sweets, Werther's Originals, and she used to give these to children we met along the way. The children were always delighted. When we parted at Bangkok I inherited the remaining sweets to give them to people I met along the way. I gave one to the young man on the bus from Siem Reap and he smiled. Today I brought some more with me to Wat Phnom. But they had an interesting effect. I gave a sweet to one young boy, perhaps around nine or ten and he declined politely. He was wise. I remember when I was growing up I was always advised not to take sweets from strange men and here I was in Phnom Penh offering sweets to these children. I was not sure I should keep giving them out but I gave one to his brother in sight of his mother. He accepted the sweet but came back five minutes later and offered me one of his orange sweets. Since I don't remember being advised not to take sweets from angelic Cambodian children at temples I took it and enjoyed his orange sweet.

I walked back to the river from the Wat and found a place to read a short version of Cambodian recent history. I had no idea that things were so bad and confused and the problems went on for so long. The troubles here are as bad as those Shakespeare represents in Henry VI with the War of the Roses. The warring factions in Cambodia lead to civil war as in Henry VI and there is no legitimate authority in the country. Unlike the English Wars of the Roses the external forces of the empires (in this case, America, China, Thailand, Vietnam and France) play a demonic role in the events in Cambodia and it is not clear there is still any resolution. These events are still alive and contemporary. In Siem Reap there are plenty of signs about the danger of landmines and there are people on the streets without limbs who are the victims of landmines.

There are plenty of figures in Cambodia who could be Richard III but in many ways, Richard III is too simple a figure. He is too easy to understand. Shakespeare is still working on the investigation of evil and Richard III is still an early example of the tyrant. The figures in Cambodia such as Sihanouk, Pol Pot and others seem far more complex but also more venal, more pedestrian and so perhaps more evil in the long run. Evil is not as interesting or as simple as Richard III.

As in Henry VI the country is rife with abuses of power, now called corruption and the national story is grabbing and maintaining power. It is not clear that Buddha has much to say about any of these problems of civil life. He opts for an inner quest and gives up on the day to day world of merchants and leaders. Perhaps his concept of compassion would help but it is not clear that he left a legacy of civil virtues and good governance. Buddha opted out of the secular sphere, like an early Prospero or like the pseudo-saintly Henry VI but this ploy did not work for Prospero nor Henry VI. In the same way that Christianity must take a share in the blame for fascism, imperial atrocities, slavery and the holocaust in Europe so Buddhism must be partly to blame for the lack of a stable civil society in this part of Indo-China.

Insight and culture has very little to contribute in the end, I suppose (there is a line from Auden's obituary of Yeats which Heaney has used as a title for a book—poetry does not matter?). In Henry VI we see the civil war in England and yet despite all the insight and understanding which Shakespeare brought to the havoc civil war brings about, England went through further civil war for a long time to come.

Let's hope Cambodia's new tower in the centre of the city is an indication of a more peaceful and prosperous future for this place and its people. It is a new mountain dedicated to the gods of business and money (and perhaps Western capitalism). I don't think Buddha would have approved but then again perhaps Buddha has had his chance and no doubt the lobby of the new tower will feature a Cambodian shrine to the

Buddha. The tower is due to open later in the year and will bring about huge change in the city.

I have had only minimal experience of the Cambodian people sadly but from those I met the people seem to be amazingly resilient despite the climate and their troubled history they are very cheerful, calm and perhaps compassionate. They don't seem to be as wracked with the fear and doubt their history may have inspired. And they have an enormous will to succeed. No doubt the current tuk tuk drivers and bicycle boys are the entrepreneurs and merchants of the future. On current evidence they have the skills and the chutzpah to thrive and survive in even trying conditions.

At the airport on the way out of Phnom Penh I found books about the South East Asian countries and their lack of a concept of the state. The academic argues that the region is governed by a stateless anarchy. And another book written by an academic from Monash university was about the role of women in Cambodia and how although they have been written out of Cambodian history they have always played a key role. This is an interesting topic. The Cambodian version of Buddhism means that there are almost no images of women in the temples and shrines, apart from the bosomy asparas. King Sihanouk chose an Italian spouse despite the supply of local aspara. The short history of Cambodia does not talk about any female political or civic leaders such as the lady in Myanmar. And yet the economic initiatives around handicrafts and quilt making and the social care initiatives around child care were driven by women. In Myanmar we saw many Buddhist nuns but in Cambodia I saw none. I don't know if they exist there.

Lazy Traveller Blog 27

27th March 2012, Bangkok Four Seasons

> "I did not count the days or weeks or the months. Time is an illusion that only makes us pant. I survived because I forgot even the very notion of time.
> What I remember are events and encounters and routines, markers that emerged here and there from the ocean of time and imprinted themselves on my memory ... But I don't know if I can put them in order for you. My memories come in a jumble."

Life of Pi, Yann Martel, (pirated copy bought in Siem Reap, omitting the author's name from the cover, p192)

I like this quotation from *Life of Pi* and perhaps it has something to do with these blogs. I have not made the connections yet but I am working on it.

Travel days are such fun when you have a good book to read as you move along. Martel's *Life of Pi* is very good. I can't say what happens in the book in case I spoil the story but the style, tone and lightness of the whole book are amazing. When I got on the plane back to Bangkok from Phnom Penh I opened my copy and started to read it. The chap sitting next to me looked over and pointed to the book he was reading. It was the same book but he said he was six chapters further on than I was. What a coincidence that we should be reading the same book and should sit next to one another on a flight of this sort! Martel would approve. Within the novel the protagonist has to tame a tiger, if he is going to survive. Because he knows how lion tamers operate in a circus and because he has grown up in a zoo in Pondicherry he has the knowledge to make this happen. He succeeds in taming the tiger and this is one of the wonders of the book. The tamer has to exert power over the tamed if they are both going to survive their ordeal. But at another level the book is also about the religious experience of its protagonist. And the author succeeds in taming his reader which puts the protagonist (or the author) back in the old role of God, a role he played until post-modernist writers decided the author did not exist. But in this novel it is clear the author does exist and he succeeds in taming his reader. He has the greater power. There is a curious and fascinating mirroring taking place within the novel between the protagonist and his tiger, the protagonist and his god, and the protagonist and the reader. This is innovative and fascinating and is delivered with the very lightest of tones which delights, amuses and draws us further into the strange enchanted world of this novel.

Yesterday morning as I was walking to the Central Market in Phnom Penh I saw something which surprised me. The monks were heading off on their morning ritual of seeking offerings. I have seen them walking around many towns in the last few weeks but I have never seen them actually accept the offerings. As I was walking down the main street I saw two monks carrying umbrellas and an offering bowl and they stopped in front of a house. This is what they do. They stand and they wait for a short period of time. I don't know if each monk has a regular circuit and the whole city is split into monkly districts. But it was clear in this case that the monk was expected and an offering was going to be made. In another instance I saw the monk stop in front of a dwelling. He stayed there for a moment with his head bowed and then he left. There was no response. No one came out to make an offering. In the case of the two monks with the umbrella a lady with someone else was ready for the two monks and they came out from the gate and made their offering. They put something into the offering bowl, i.e. food of some sort. The monks responded by chanting for a moment or two. This was the surprise. I had no idea how the monks responded to an offering. They sing or chant. They receive the offering and respond with a song, a prayer of thanksgiving perhaps to which the person making the offering responds by bowing their head just as the monk bowed his head before the offering was made. It was a good moment to witness, a private intimate moment between the person making the offering and everything which the monks represented. I was so pleased to have the opportunity to see this small street ritual.

"We cast a shadow on something wherever we stand." E. M. Forster says. This is another quotation I found today and like very much. These blogs are about the shadow cast as I have moved around for the last few weeks. These quotations begin to define the purpose and outcome of the blogs retrospectively.

Today in Bangkok I decided to have an easy day and do things which I have already enjoyed. I went for a trip down the Chao Phraya. It is good to see the city of Bangkok from the perspective of the river. I have now visited a number of these South East Asian cities but Bangkok is probably the most beautiful. The river is not as large as the Mekong and both banks are filled with a huge range of delights: old buildings, temples and stupas, markets, boat stops, modern splendid hotels and new apartment and office blocks and there is still a lot of life on the river itself with small ferries crossing back and forth from one side of the river to another constantly. When I did this trip a few weeks ago this was all new to me. Now my eyes could see more of what was in front of them. It was interesting to see the Chinese quarter loom and realise that the Chinese influence is a speciality of Thailand. It is not as strong in Myanmar or Cambodia (despite the Maoist project to return Cambodia to a rural agrarian society and to banish everyone from the cities). It was interesting to see Wat Arun again on the bank. The structure is not just a single stupa but like Angkor Wat it contains a large main stupa and four stupas at each cardinal point. In effect the temple complex repeats the pattern of the temple mountain range of the five sacred mountains from Anghor Wat. Originally Wat Arun was a Royal Temple and contained the Emerald Buddha which has now migrated across the river to the Royal Palace. Wat Arun is decorated with porcelain fragments which shine in the morning sunshine and give it a colour and delicacy which I have seen on no other stupa on this trip. It is special.

On the other bank the Royal Palace suddenly looms up and again it is easier to judge this palace complex now in the light of Phnom Penh and Mandalay and the Palace complex in Bangkok is the best. It is the most graceful, the most elegant, the one with more colours than the others. It is a wonder even of its type. I did not want to visit it again but it was good to see the different stupas arising from the palace walls and realise again how splendid this complex is, probably the best.

I thought I was going to find a Buddha to bring back to the UK. I saw many stalls on my first day sight-seeing when I accidentally walked into a street market full of Buddha images and images of old abbots and wise men. Tim and Reid always come back with many of these images carefully selected. But I looked and I looked and no Buddha seemed to be asking to come back with me to London. I was willing to give up on a Buddha and just go for a wise old man. Perhaps that is what the house now needs, not a Buddha. But the wise old men and abbots were not that interested in making the journey back to London tomorrow. I came away empty handed.

However, there is a Buddha on the balcony of Weston Park, given to me by my parents or my sister a few years ago. He is a large fat smiling middle aged Buddha, the sort of Buddha you find in China but not in South East Asia. He is the Buddha which greets temple visitors in China in the first audience hall. He is a Buddha of gracious plenty, contentment and liberal hospitality. He is fecund and sometimes he is represented with small children climbing over his fat tummy. Since I have such a good Buddha perhaps I don't need another one.

I returned to Loha Prasat to see if this place which I originally thought so wonderful would retain its magic this morning. It did. As if to echo the image which struck me the day before at the stupa in Phnom Penh a lady was down on the ground delousing the ears of another dog. And a saffron robed monk was having tea while playing with his attentive dog close by.

It was great to wander around each floor, moving from one to the next using the spiral staircase at its centre, the only staircase in the whole building. Unlike the elaborate structures I have seen elsewhere this is starkly simple. It is all straight lines, squares built on squares, corridors of simple proportions. It is an exercise in very simple but lucid geometry and yet it is wonderfully cool and sheltered. It rises to five or six layers and yet it is of human proportions. There are Buddha images on two levels but all of these are less than life size. There is no gigantism here. No flashing neon. Not even mirrors and coloured glass. This is a building where monks came during the rainy season, when the rest of the country is occupied with the rain, to make a retreat, and in this time of the rainy season be further formed in the discipline of their chosen lifestyle. They would aim to move from one floor to the next, to become more disciplined and more enlightened in their practice.

The building was even clearer and more lucid than I remembered. This is a house of formation as well as a house of wisdom. The walls contain sayings of the Buddha which help to form the monks. The building itself enshrines the core teachings and disciplines of Buddha with its library, its floor for walking meditation and another for sitting meditation, a floor which looks out over the city and the relic chamber at the top of the building houses the relics of the Buddha. The teachings are about how to develop the will, how to form an inner character. Buddha is a psychologist, concerned to provide clear direction and focus. It is a stark, strong and clear message, rigorously rational and humanist. Each floor reinforces key skills required to pull away from the shadows and civil war of egotism, desire and aggression and build wisdom, character, mastery over the mind and a focus on compassion. Buddha is not interested in the art of eros but only has an interest in creating the prerequisites for compassion or agape.

It was very good to return to Bangkok last night. There is no difference in the climate between Myanmar, Cambodia and Thailand and yet Thailand and Bangkok are so much easier places than these others. I could feel this even before I arrived at the hotel. It was clear from the moment we landed at the airport. Life was easier. Things worked again and worked simply. Trains, tickets, signs, roads. Nothing was very complicated. Foreigners were not special anymore and this felt very good. I suppose what underlies this comfort is that Thailand feels a more equal country than these other places and countries with higher levels of equality feel easier to deal with.

I am not sure that the level of equality, measured in some way or other, is actually better here but it certainly feels that way or perhaps I mean that Thailand feels a wealthier country. But I don't know that the level of comfort would increase just because of the wealth. Thailand has invested in making the city habitable for everyone.

In Myanmar and Cambodia foreigners are deemed to be super wealthy and sources of hard currency. We become targets, carrion for local skilful vultures, in various disguises and we in turn become vultures seeking to take more than we give. In some way we are granted too much power (economic power) and that skews every other relationship. The people are very friendly and it is easy to see how comfortable these places are for their own people but severe inequality makes it impossible as a foreigner to relax. It is possible to cope and everything is designed to make things go well and they do go well. But it is great to pull away at the end and land back in somewhere such as Bangkok where the relations between people seem different.

The new Bangkok Art and Cultural Centre across from the National Stadium and Madame Tussaud's was a complete surprise. This is a contemporary stunning nine-floor landmark building. This is a big statement from the outside, from its location and from the amazing structures internally. It is a vast space full of light and yet shaded and cool with a fascinating series of elevators and spiral staircases wandering up this tube-like structure, while on the outside it looks like a concrete box. I wonder who the architect was. It is on the same scale as the Beaubourg in Paris or Tate Modern. I am not sure when it opened. It feels very new and it also feels as if the curators are still struggling to find the right material to put into it. When I visited there was a large exhibition on AIDS in the main gallery, a photographic exhibition by a French artist and a series on Shadow lives from Aboriginal Indians. But still, after all the traditional and museum culture I have had for the last month it was very good to see contemporary work created by people who are not monks and who are outside a formal and traditional structure attempting to deal with complex issues. This trip has been about cultural monuments to an old traditional and Buddhist culture which is clearly in decline in power and influence. It has not been about seeing the new buds of an emerging culture. If Bangkok is going to be the centre of ASEAN innovation and creativity that it aspires to be for this century it needs to have the institutions to cultivate and promote new conversations about issues that matter. This new Art and Cultural Centre may be one indication of the future, quite unlike the contemporary but traditional art gallery I visited last week where the art was very parochial and undemanding.

Lazy Traveller Blog 28

28th March 2012, Bangkok Four Seasons and flight back to London via Bahrain

I am on the flight returning from Bangkok to London, via Bahrain. The holiday is over. It has been so good. I am full of gratitude and pleasure about how good it was, and also feel a little sadness, that it is all over.

The people of course are the big stars of vacations. The people we travel with, those we remain in touch with, new people we meet, angelic supporters who step in to guide us on our way, new figures who appear in person or culturally. The people of Thailand, Myanmar and Cambodia proved endlessly fascinating to look at, to watch, to listen to and to learn from. This sort of speedy vacation does not lead to in depth explorations but it is fascinating and delightful to look, to watch and to pay attention to those around us.

Karen Armstrong highlights a distinction found in Gabriel Marcel. "The French philosopher ... distinguished between a *problem*, 'something met which bars my passage', and 'is before me in its entirety,' and a *mystery*, 'something in which I find myself caught up, and whose essence is not before me in its entirety.' We have to remove a problem before we can proceed, but we are compelled to participate in a mystery—rather as the Greeks flung themselves into the rites of Eleusis and grappled with their mortality. 'A mystery is something in which I am myself involved.' Marcel continued, 'and it can therefore only be thought of as *a sphere where the distinction between what is in me and what is before me loses its meaning and its essential validity.*'" Travels to new and foreign countries comprise part problem, the easy part, and part mystery, the elusive, intriguing and challenging part. The problem aspect can sometimes dominate and consume a lot of energy but in the end both the problems and their resolutions are trivial. Mysteries cannot be solved. Initially they demand less attention. They can even go unnoticed because they are silent. They seem so less demanding than the problems. We can only participate in them (and get lost in their confusion). These blogs involve a lot of noise about the problems and, to some small extent, they become an attempt to notice the mysteries and to respect their outlines, if not to plumb their depths. Countries, cultures and other people are mysteries we try to relate to and open ourselves to be changed by our relationship with them.

And if that is not what these blogs do, perhaps it is what they should have done. Perhaps their goal has only emerged with time and only becomes clear at the end, as with so many things in life. Endings are helpful to gain perspective and understanding. Reflection at some distance from the fray is required for understanding.

Perhaps they start consumed by a sense of the problems involved in this journey and they end finally with a better understanding of the mysteries the journey has involved. The journey has been an exploration into the mysteries of the countries visited and some small participation in their cultural heritage.

"All journeys have secret destinations of which the traveller is unaware" Martin Buber said at one stage, as quoted in a Guardian article about Cambodia.

It was good to have this time away from the UK, to relax and see the world anew, to see a new world and new countries, to see so much. Vacations, such as this, provide an opportunity to change, to be touched by the world, and in response to the new outer world find new inner resources, in effect to discover ourselves anew. And holidays can bring about a sort of transformation. They enable the pieces of who we are to be pulled apart for a while and then they can be reassembled in a new combination. And if the alchemy works well the new combination is likely to be more consistent with the outside world and our new sense of our own skills and potential. We can hope for an increased radiance (as well as a sun tan), for the new combination to be more fitting, calling upon more of our inner resources. That is the hope.

And just as pilgrimages are journeys away from the ordinary to new (but old) places of power, places of origin and creativity so a vacation can be a journey back to our own source, a centre of power, vitality and possibly creativity. That is another aspect of the hope, the motivation for heading off on such a journey.

And this journey was undertaken in a year of personal renewal and refreshment, a sabbatical year, a year involved in ending one phase of life which started in China in 2005 while preparing for the next phase, whatever that might involve. It was undertaken in the middle of a much longer, year long, project about Shakespeare. And it was undertaken a few weeks after a few days in Tenby when I did some work on the topic of love, based on the writings of Erich Fromm, Rilke, Rumi and Comte-Sponville. I suppose the context creates the questions we are mulling over as we undertake this sort of journey.

It may take a few weeks to distil the outcome of the journey and see how the experiences and impressions of the last few weeks relate to this overall context. I thought I was going to be able to write about these things tonight but now I realise dinner will be served shortly and my mind is focused on food and sleep. I write better in the morning. By a certain time of the evening my resources are depleted.

I want to thank those of you have been daily recipients of these notes. It has been good to share the journey with you and to hear back your comments. I want to thank Cornelia for planning the Myanmar journey, for making so many good decisions and for being such a good companion. Tim and Reid lent me their guidebooks to Thailand and to Cambodia and gave me many helpful suggestions. Ciara's blog of her far longer journey around the world provided inspiration and Rachel gave me hints and tips about Cambodia. Hints and tips a lazy traveller always finds useful if not essential.

These notes over the last few weeks are just impressions, comments and musings. They have not been validated nor checked so they contain many errors and mistakes. And for the most part I have not had time to write as well as edit them. Apologies. There is never enough time to correct typos and do a final draft.

This is the first time that I have written one of these travel blogs, inspired by Ciara's example. Her blog kept us all informed of where she was and what she was up to while she was away for four months. Her inspiration gave me the idea to write something daily. They were fun to write. After a while a concept of what to include and write about became clearer. I would not give a narrative of what happened but I would focus on just a few of the surprises which had occurred on that day. For Myanmar Cornelia and I would share our list of surprises towards the evening. We would often have different lists but it was always a good way to end the day, reflecting on what had happened and how what happened surprised us. Writing these notes has proved that it is very hard to write about lots of things. It is hard to write about food, birds, history, architecture. I need more practice and I am going back to read examples from those who write well about these things.

Now there is joy at the prospect of getting back home, tiredness, exhilaration at all that has happened over the four weeks and the many surprises that appeared on the way. And there is also a sense of sadness that the journey has finally come to

THE END.

17635891R00123

Printed in Poland
by Amazon Fulfillment
Poland Sp. z o.o., Wrocław